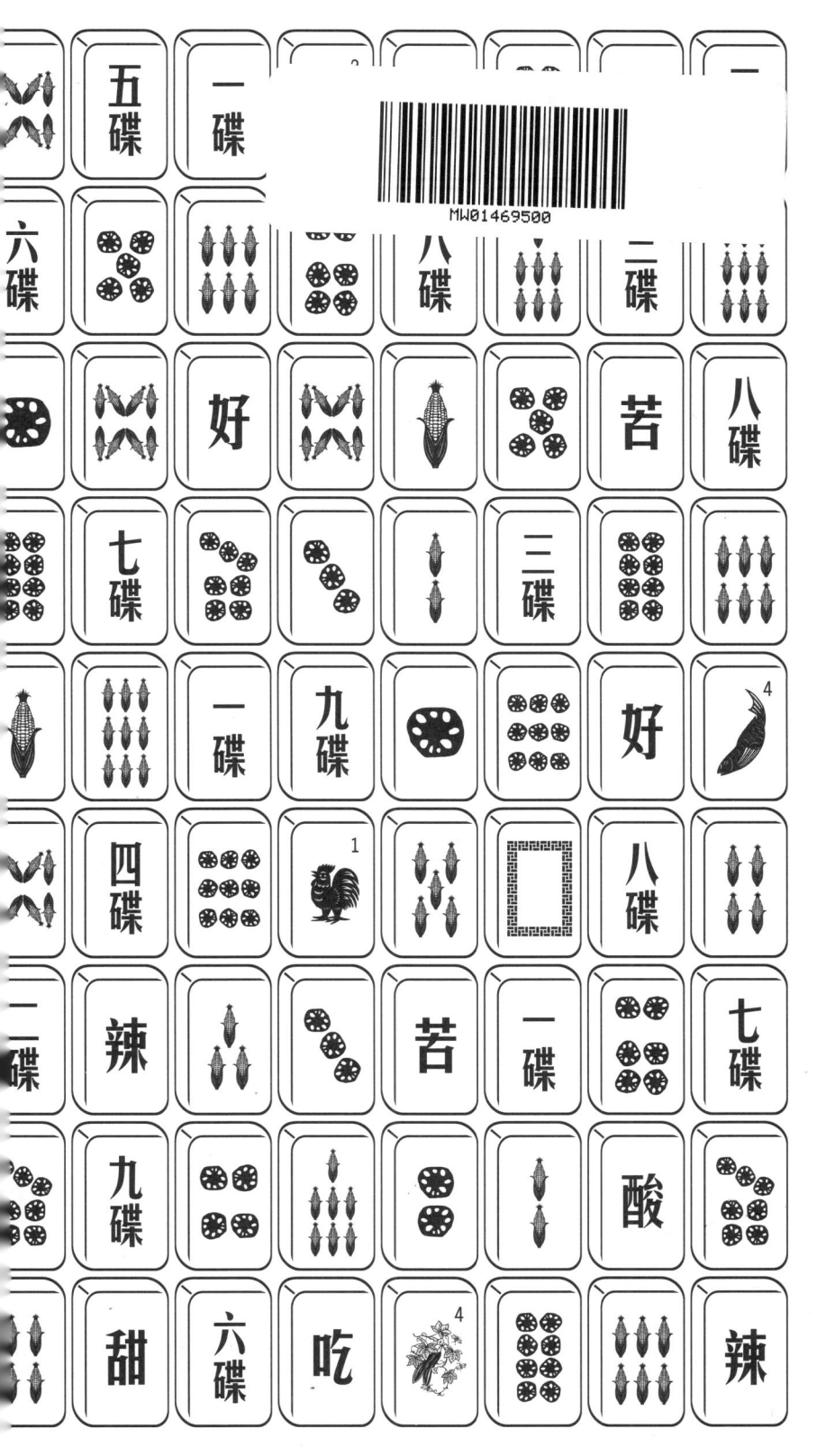

🌽🌽	五碟	一碟					一
六碟	🪷🪷	🌽🌽🌽	🪷🪷	八碟	🌽🌽🌽	二碟	🌽🌽🌽
🪷	🌽🌽	好	🌽🌽	🌽	🪷🪷🪷	若	八碟
🪷🪷🪷	七碟	🪷🪷	🪷🪷	🌽	三碟	🪷🪷🪷	🌽🌽🌽
🌽	🌽🌽🌽	一碟	九碟	🪷	🪷🪷🪷	好	🐟⁴
🌽🌽	四碟	🪷🪷🪷	🐓¹	🌽🌽	▢	八碟	🌽🌽
二碟	辣	🌽🌽	🪷🪷	若	一碟	🪷🪷🪷	七碟
🪷🪷	九碟	🪷🪷	🌽🌽🌽	🪷	🌽	酸	🪷🪷🪷
🌽	甜	六碟	吃	🌶⁴	🪷🪷🪷	🌽🌽🌽	辣

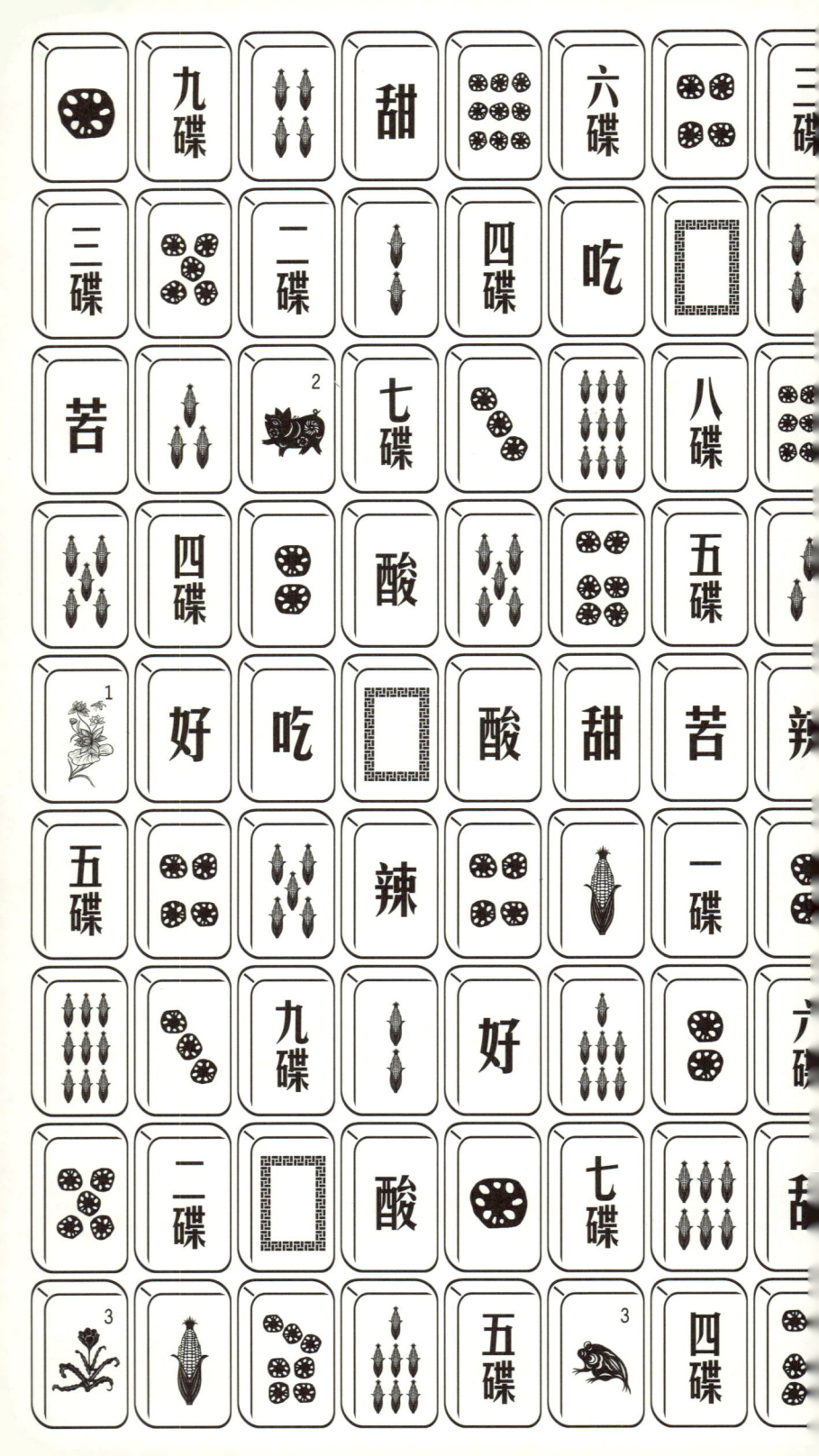

藕	九碟	玉米	甜	藕	六碟	藕	三碟
三碟	藕	二碟	玉米	四碟	吃	▢	玉米
苦	玉米	猪²	七碟	藕	玉米	八碟	藕
玉米	四碟	藕	酸	玉米	藕	五碟	玉米
花¹	好	吃	▢	酸	甜	苦	辣
五碟	藕	玉米	辣	藕	玉米	一碟	藕
玉米	藕	九碟	玉米	好	玉米	藕	六碟
藕	二碟	▢	酸	藕	七碟	玉米	甜
花³	玉米	藕	玉米	五碟	鼠³	四碟	藕

madam choy's cantonese recipes

Other books in the Heritage Cookbook series

irene's peranakan recipes
robin's eurasian recipes
madam krishnan's south indian recipes
uncle lau's teochew recipes
uncle anthony's hokkien recipes

madam choy's cantonese recipes

EPIGRAM BOOKS

wok of life

"Dining out is unnecessary expense."
Food was my mother's way of pampering us.

A veritable housewife
choy wai yuen

MY MOTHER WAS BORN 85 years ago in Kuala Lumpur of parents who emigrated from Guangdong province in China. They would soon move to Seremban, in the Malaysian state of Negri Sembilan, where eleven other children followed in quick succession. Only seven, including my mother, survived and the family occupied the corner terrace house just outside the town where my grandfather became a prominent businessman. Besides the family, there were several *mui jye*, young bonded maids from China who came with my grandmother when she got married, a handful of adopted daughters, and in later years, several servants hired from the town.

The Chooi household (my mother's surname was changed to Choy by an inept bureaucrat) was large and noisy, under the command and control of my grandmother. The children led carefree lives while being educated in schools that put little if any pressure on them. The elder daughters were matched in their mid-teens with prospective husbands and the boys were sent to prestigious schools in Penang and groomed to take over the family business.

The dinner table was always bountiful, and soon every family member was a food critic commenting on every mouthful, from simple snacks to exquisite banquet dishes. It was little wonder that my mother soon learned what good food was. But with maids and servants handling all the work, she did nothing in the kitchen and showed little interest, and never learned even to boil water!

At 16, my mother, then a slip of a girl and still in school, married my father, Loke Seck Cheong, and moved to Singapore, where she found herself in a terrace house off Jalan Besar. Here, my paternal grandmother ruled the house, including the kitchen, a tiny cubicle with a charcoal stove. A stern matriarch who doted on her son and grandsons, Grandma Loke discussed the daily menu with our black-and-white amah, *ng chay* (fifth sister). Breakfast before school was rice with fish, meat and vegetables. Ham was unheard of, although my father had three soft-boiled eggs every morning, a practice that stopped when cholesterol crept into our vocabulary. Daily meals were simple but tasty enough.

Back in Seremban, the situation was the complete opposite. At year's end every year after the War, my mother took us – two girls and two boys – to Seremban to join our numerous cousins, who had grown in number after another aunt and uncle got married. Grandma and Second Aunt who married Mother's younger brother, with help from two maids and the now-elderly former maids who visited frequently, churned out huge meals several times a day. Visiting daughters like my mother would help in simple tasks. Together, they served up mid-morning and afternoon snacks and supper, plus the three main meals. As the extended brood grew, it became clear the tiny kitchen between the inner hall and the toilet at the back was inadequate.

Around the late 1950s, Grandpa Chooi bought the empty land next to the house and built an enormous kitchen the size of a small flat. It had a row of burners, a big round table that could seat a dozen or more, and numerous storage shelves and cupboards. Here, the women folk gathered to peel and pluck, stir-fry and simmer to feed the holidaying hordes at regular meal times and in between. This was when we kids picked up the art of food tasting.

Second Uncle had the most discerning palate and would comment on every dish. Even the cow's milk, delivered each morning in bottles by dhoti-clad men on bicycles, then boiled and served salted or sweetened slightly, was deemed either "rich and full-bodied" or "flat and not fragrant". Others would pitch in, especially when the food was below par.

From the time we third-generation children could walk and talk, we had learned that texture and fragrance were as important to food as taste. Noodles should "spring off the teeth" (*darn ngah*) which is more descriptive than the Italian *al dente*. Fried dishes must have *wok hei*, long before western food writers called it the "breath of the wok". Steamed fish should be smooth (*waht*) and just cooked, indicated by a slight redness near the bone. The dough of prawn dumplings (*har gau*) should be translucent and springy, and not stick to the teeth. Shark's fins, in those pre-conservation days, should have sufficiently firm body (*gau sun*) which meant a bite that was not hard like a stick of carrot nor soft like jelly, and different from *darn ngah* noodles. And the crackling of roast suckling pig must have a light crispness (*soong chooi*). We also knew that sweet (*teem*) was not necessarily sugary and *gum*, which sounded like the word for gold, was a tangy taste that had no equivalent in English.

Street and fast foods were not spared; from roadside apom pancakes to A&W's curly-cue fries, they all came under scrutiny. One house specialty was love letters, the crisp coconut and egg biscuits, made every year as gifts for the Chinese New Year. The production line was set up in the air well. Three open charcoal fires baked the paper-thin sheets in three flat cast-iron clams, operated by three aunts or maids for days on end. Each sheet would be peeled from the open clam and folded with a chopstick into triangles and fitted into large Milo tins. When cool, they were feather light, and when bitten, released a wonderful coconut fragrance. The sheets were so fragile that when rolled into cigar shapes, they broke easily in the tins. Family connoisseurs would walk by and grab a handful "to make sure they were of the usual high standard" they claimed. Today, no store-bought love letters can match those – in texture or fragrance.

During the durian season, Second Uncle would come home with an industrial-sized basket of the spiky fruit and Grandpa would open them one at a time. Uncle would taste a seed from the first fruit and comment on the fragrance, texture and taste. If it was deemed good, we would all dive in. If not, the whole fruit would be tossed aside and another cracked open. Durians that were not overly ripe were described as having yellow flesh in a dry pouch (*wong yoke gon bau*). Small, shrunken seeds were known as seed-sucking good (*jueet wut*). Bitter-sweet (*foo teem*) was an acquired taste and came only from good durians. If the flesh was wet (*siok*), unripe (*sarng bau*) or bland (*tarm*), it would be discarded. One by one, the whole basket of durians would be polished off with the rejects untouched.

Back in Singapore, meals remained the predictable meat, fish and vegetables, until 1957 when we moved to a big house with a long, large kitchen. It had sky-blue cabinets that reached the ceiling, a double sink at one end, a gas hob with an oven below, and a round marble-top table that could seat six. For the first time, my mother felt she had a kitchen of her own. The meek newly-wed girl had meanwhile grown into a confident, though less svelte, woman and began experimenting with dishes she had learned from Seremban. Together with a neighbour, an excellent cook who made melt-in-the-mouth Swiss rolls, my mother went to cooking classes. She kept recipes from newspapers and magazines, expanding her repertoire by adapting them to her own taste.

While *ng chay* continued to produce the standard fare, my mother began turning out fancy dishes like double-boiled soup with whole chicken stuffed with bird's nest for special occasions. Whenever there was steamed chicken or braised duck, it would be one of our birthdays (but no cakes and candles nor presents). The dinner table would be covered with dishes, almost always with a soup. When we had dinner guests, the finest crockery was brought out and the meal would be a *tour de force* that left us groaning. But we were not allowed to moan that we were full. Grandma would scold us as being *moh yee sek* which meant something like "lacking in eating decorum."

Looking back, I think we took for granted some of the most delicious dishes that my mother no longer makes today because of the high cost. Among these are chicken with cordyceps soup, braised abalones in oyster sauce, and bird's nest soup. They are included in this book for those with deep pockets. Until just a few years ago, the highlight of my mother's culinary year was the Chinese New Year reunion dinner which always included shark's fin soup. Nature conservation awareness has put paid to this family favourite, which has been replaced by bamboo fungus. The preparation of the fins from the dried whole fin into crunchy golden strands is a pain-staking process and is not described here for the same reason shark's fin soup is left out.

Mother's skills in the kitchen were not her only assets. A veritable housewife, she was among the first women in Singapore to earn a driver's licence in the early 1950s, zipping around in her black Morris Minor driving us to and from school. She sewed all my sister's and my clothes, including our school uniforms, and curtains for the new house and planted beds of orchids in the garden. She managed the big two-storey detached house with just one elderly maid and a part-time gardener.

With four growing children, she made sure we toed the line and was a strict disciplinarian. Speaking only a smattering of English words, she must have been frustrated when her children rattled in an incomprehensible language that she had tried but failed to learn. Perhaps because of her own conservative upbringing, she was at a loss when it came to her children's social life. More out of fear than disapproval, she frowned on single dates, worse when with a non-Chinese, as was my Eurasian boyfriend. Afraid of the possible clash of culture and language, she objected vehemently, until Grandma Loke, the domineering matriarch who had mellowed into a frail old woman, approved. When we were married, as if her objections never happened, my mother doted on my husband and would prepare his favourite dishes at family dinners.

Food was my mother's way of pampering us. Anything we asked for would appear on the dinner table. Today, sadly, my mother's bad back has reduced her cooking to a minimum, supervising the maid rather than picking up the spatula herself. With four married children, seven grandchildren and five great-grandchildren – and more on their way – she can no longer cope with family dinners. Reluctantly, and after years of protests against "unnecessary expense", she now agrees to hold Chinese New Year reunion dinners in a restaurant.

Learning to cook from my mother is frustrating. To her, cooking is more art than science; nothing is measured and every ingredient is added by instinct. Some ingredients are optional, depending on one's preference. "More or less" or "up to you" were her frequent replies to my queries on the portions. Or she would say "one dollar's worth should be enough". She constantly tasted what she was cooking as she went along, adjusting the seasoning, making it difficult to know exactly how much salt or sauce she was using. For some dishes, she would stick her finger into a bowl of raw meat and suck the finger to test the seasoning, a habit that would horrify food hygienists.

The measurements in these recipes are just a guide. To find out the proportions that suit you, try the recipe and adjust the seasoning to your liking. Even the size of the servings is subjective because a dish could feed two or ten, depending on what else is on the dining table.

Apart from the proportions, the quality of the ingredients and seasoning can affect the taste. Mother would swear by particular brands of soya sauce or rice flour. Choosing food items is another skill that goes beyond fish with bright red gills. For instance, bitter gourds with broad ridges are less bitter. I have tried to include as many of these tips as possible.

There are other tips on getting the correct texture and taste such as in the braising of sea cucumber and the seasoning of mushrooms. Some instructions are difficult to describe, such as the wrapping of rice dumplings (*jung*). Without watching her do it, or a video, the only way to find out is to buy one from the market and open it carefully to see how the bamboo leaves are wrapped around the filling and tied.

Getting the Cantonese terms for ingredients and dishes was also a problem, until help came from my sister Loo Pin. Together we managed to name them all, albeit with some unconventional transliterations.

My family owes my mother a great debt for all the fabulous meals she produced, but nothing makes her happier than to see people enjoy her cooking. When discussing this book with her, she was often self-deprecating and brushed aside any suggestion that anyone would want to try her recipes. I hope you will prove her wrong.

Lulin Reutens
December 2007

Contents

Soups
- Superior Stock 2
- Fish Stock 3
- Bamboo Fungus Soup 4
- Chicken Herbal Soup 5
- Black Chicken Soup 6
- Snow Fungus Chicken Soup 7
- Top Shell Soup 8
- Bird's Nest Chicken Soup 9
- Abalone Chicken Soup 10
- Beancurd Stick Soup 11
- Cordyceps Soup ...12
- Lotus Root Soup ..13
- Salted Vegetable Soup 14
- Three-coloured Carrot Soup 15
- Old Cucumber Soup 16
- Watercress Soup ..17
- Winter Melon Soup 18
- Pig's Brains Soup ...20
- Pig's Stomach Soup 21
- Pig's Liver Soup ...22
- Cream of Winter Melon Soup 23

Poultry
- White Chopped Chicken 26
- Chicken in Dark Soya Sauce............27
- Crispy Skin Chicken 28
- Braised Chicken with Potatoes 29
- Braised Chicken Feet 30
- Salt Baked Chicken 32
- Sesame Chicken 33
- Chicken and Ham Roll 34
- Chicken with Cloud-ear Fungus..............36
- Paper-wrapped Chicken 37
- Chicken Wings in Prawn Paste...........38
- Braised Duck with Yam 39
- Lotus Duck 40

Pork
- Mother-in-law Eggs 46
- Hakka Pork Balls 47
- Minced Pork Steamed with Salted Fish 48
- Pork Ribs and Bitter Gourd in Black Bean Sauce 49
- Pig's Trotters in Black Vinegar 50
- Sweet Sour Pork....51
- Crispy Roast Pork 52
- Roast Pork Ribs 53
- Fried Pig's Liver ...54
- Pork and Prawn Dumplings 55
- Pork Belly in Dark Soya Sauce 56

Seafood
- Steamed Pomfret.................60
- Fried Garoupa 61
- Batang Fish Steaks 62
- Fried Tiger Prawns 63
- Prawns with Bell Peppers...........64
- Cuttlefish with Broccoli 65
- Steamed Crabs 66
- Fish Maw Stew......67
- Stuffed Clams 68
- Fish Slices with Mustard Greens ...69
- Fish Cake in Beancurd Skin 70
- Braised Sea Cucumber...............71
- Abalone in Oyster Sauce 72

madam choy's cantonese recipes

Published by Epigram Books
www.epigrambooks.sg
Copyright © 2007, 2015 Epigram Books. All rights reserved. No part of this publication may be reproduced without prior consent from the publisher.
Printed in Singapore.

National Library Board Singapore Cataloguing in Publication Data
Choy, Wai Yuen, 1922-
    Madam Choy's Cantonese Recipes.– Singapore : Epigram, 2007.
    p. cm.
    ISBN-13 : 978-981-05-9402-2

    1. Cookery, Chinese – Cantonese style. I. Title. II. Title : Madam Choy's Cantonese Recipes
TX724.5.C5
641.595127 -- dc22   OCN174152424

First Edition
10 9 8 7 6 5 4

E
EPIGRAM BOOKS

Vegetables

Boxthorn in Superior Stock 78
Hair Seaweed with Cloud-Ear Fungus 79
Mushrooms with Oyster Sauce 80
Hairy Marrow with Vermicelli 81
Stuffed Hairy Marrow 82
Bitter Gourd Omelette 84
Fried Snow Peas....85
Potato Cakes 86
Lettuce Pouches ...87
Chinese New Year Raw Fish 88
Fried Egg Packets 90
Crab Omelette 91
Three-egg Steamed Custard 92
Beancurd with Prawn Roe 93
Beancurd Skin Rolls 94
Stuffed Dried Beancurd 95
Eight Treasures Beancurd 96
Stuffed Bitter Gourd.....................97
Stuffed Brinjals.....98

Rice & Noodles

Fried Rice 122
Glutinous Rice ...103
One-pot Chicken Rice 104
Chicken Congee 105
Rice Dumplings 106
Egg Noodles 108
Rat Noodles 110

Savoury Snacks

Beancurd Stick Rolls 112
Yam Cake 114
Radish Cake........115
Chinese Potato Crisps...................116

Desserts

Steamed Egg Custard 120
Red Beans Soup 121
Black Sesame Soup 122
Lotus Seeds Soup 123
Double-boiled Snow Fungus 124
Jade Dessert 125
Sweet Potato Soup 126
Gingko Nuts with Soya Bean Sticks..........127
Glutinous Rice Balls 128
Soya Milk 129
Water Chestnut Cake 130
New Year Cake ...131
Hasma Sweet Soup 132

Soups

SUPERIOR STOCK
SIONG TONG

This is the basic stock for almost every dish that requires a sauce. Make a big pot and freeze it in half-cup portions in plastic containers. Just melt one container's contents for making the sauce. Or melt 2 or more cups for a soup. For daily use, you may use store-bought stock in packets or tins, or chicken cubes in hot water, although they don't have the same intense flavour and most of them have MSG.

- 2-3 chicken breasts, blanched, skin removed
- 2-3 slices of Chinese Kam Wah ham or 1-2 ham bones, blanched
- 4 dried scallops, soaked and shredded; keep the water
- salt and pepper

Put all ingredients and the soaking water into a large pot and add enough water to cover the ingredients. Bring to boil and reduce the heat. Cover and simmer for 3 hours.

Skim off the froth and oil. Remove the ingredients and strain the stock through a sieve into another pot. Season to taste.

You may vary the intensity of the stock by using more chicken breasts or water.

Tips

Chicken breasts are used here only because they are more convenient and cheap. Mother would use "old chicken" when cooking for special occasions. They are larger than the average chicken and cost more. Ask for them at chicken stalls in wet markets. Skin the chicken and cut it into four and cook as instructed above.

Dried scallops are among the most costly Chinese dried seafood; the largest specimens of about 3cm in diameter cost hundreds of dollars a kilo, and have the sweetest and most intense taste and flavour. Fortunately, there are smaller ones which are more affordable, right down to tiny ones which are cheap enough to use by the handfuls.

Kam Wah ham is a delicacy, used in small amounts because of the saltiness but it has a heavenly flavour. If unavailable, leave it out. Do not replace with smoked ham hock as it has a different taste.

𝒫3/
FISH STOCK
YU GUAT TONG

This can be used as the base for noodle soup or other seafood stews.

- 3 cm piece of ginger, cut into strips
- 5-6 shallots, finely chopped
- 5-6 garlic, finely chopped
- 3 snakefish bones, about 1kg, cut into 10cm pieces
- oil for frying
- 6-7 cups water
- 1 tsp chicken granules, optional

Heat some oil in a wok and fry the ginger, shallots and garlic over high heat till light brown and fragrant.

Add the fish bones and fry till brown. Add enough water to cover the bones, cover the wok and bring to boil. Reduce the heat and simmer for about an hour until the stock is opaque.

Strain the stock into another pot. Add another 3 or 4 cups of water to the residue in the wok and repeat the process to extract more taste from the bones. Add the second lot of stock to the first and strain it all through a fine sieve or muslin cloth. Season to taste.

Variation

The stock is great for making Rice Vermicelli Soup with Fish Slices (yu peen mye fun). Here's how: Soak some rice vermicelli in water. Simmer a cup of fish stock in a pot and cook slices of snakehead meat or threadfin (mar yau) in it for under a minute. Add the noodles and mustard greens (choy sum), bring to a boil and season with soya sauce, sesame oil and pepper. That's it!

P4/Soups
BAMBOO FUNGUS SOUP
JOKE SUN TONG

This has replaced shark's fin soup in our family dinners. The crunchy texture of bamboo fungus more than compensates for the fins, and is far easier to prepare.

- 10 g dried bamboo fungus
- 4 cups superior stock
- cooked meat from ½ crab
- 1 egg
- 1 tbs starch mixed with 2 tbs water
- 1 tbs red crab roe, optional
- salt and pepper

Simmer the bamboo fungus in water for 10 minutes. Drain and squeeze dry, and cut the pieces of fungus into strips. Discard the water.

Add the fungus to the stock in a large pot and bring to a boil. Beat an egg with 2-3 tablespoons of water or stock and stir into the stock over high heat, stirring all the time.

With the soup simmering, add the starch-mixture a little at a time, stirring all the while. Stop when the soup begins to thicken and continue to simmer for a few more minutes. Stir in the crab meat. Season to taste.

Transfer into a soup tureen or individual soup bowls. Garnish with crab roe before serving.

Tip
Bamboo fungus, also known as bamboo pith, is very light weight and is sold in packets. Each stalk consists of a stem section topped with a floral-like section. Mother chooses the yellowish variety which has a very short floral section. It costs more than the paler variety but has a more crunchy texture.

Variation
Add pieces of raw chicken meat cut from a chicken thigh and a handful of blanched bean sprouts for a more substantial soup. Black vinegar, often added to shark's fin soup, is not recommended here.

CHICKEN HERBAL SOUP
DUN GYE TONG

This soup is comfort food at its best, with an intensely herbal richness without being medicinal. It is the quintessential Cantonese soup. You may vary the taste by changing the kind and amount of herbs.

- 3 chicken breasts with bone, or 1 medium-sized old chicken, skinned and cut into chunks
- 15 red dates, blanched and deseeded
- ¼ cup dried longan, blanched
- 3-4 strips astragalus, blanched
- 30 g ginseng beard, blanched
- 1 tbs wolfberries
- 5-6 pieces dioscorea
- 1 tbs ferox nuts, optional
- 1 tbs dried lily bulbs
- 5-6 dried scallops, soaked and shredded; keep the water
- 50 g Chinese sweet almonds, soaked and peeled, optional
- salt and pepper

Put all the ingredients into a double-boiler and add enough water to cover the contents. Double-boil for 4 hours.

If you don't have a double-boiler, use a large pot. Bring to boil and reduce heat. Cover the pot, leaving a small gap to prevent it from boiling over and simmer for 3-4 hours. Season to taste.

Tips

Red dates give the soup a sweetness, so use fewer if you prefer it less sweet.

Large dried scallops of about 3cm diameter are very expensive. For use in a daily soup, the smaller variety of about ½cm diameter will do, although the big ones do give a rich flavour.

Chinese herbs are usually labelled with their western names but in the market or medicine shops, ask for them by their Chinese names. See Glossary.

BLACK CHICKEN SOUP
HARK GYE TONG

Black chicken is supposed to be more nourishing than white chicken, and especially good for postpartum women. The herbs are similar to those used for herbal chicken soup. Ginseng slices may be used instead of ginseng beard for additional goodness.

- 1 black chicken, about 1kg, skinned
- 10 red dates, blanched and deseeded
- 1 tbs wolfberries
- 5-6 pieces dioscorea
- 30 g ginseng beard or thin slices of ginseng, blanched
- 5-6 dried scallops, soaked and shredded; keep the water
- salt and pepper

Put all the ingredients into a double-boiler and add enough water to cover the contents. Double-boil for 4 hours.

If you don't have a double-boiler, use a large pot. Bring to boil. Reduce the heat and simmer for 3-4 hours. Season to taste.

SNOW FUNGUS CHICKEN SOUP
SHUIT YEE GYE TONG

Once you have made your superior stock, this is the easiest soup to make. Plus, snow fungus has a nice crispy crunch.

- 100 g snow fungus, soaked and cleaned
- 3-4 cups superior stock
- soya sauce
- salt and pepper

Break the snow fungus into pieces. Simmer in water for 1 minute and discard the water.

Add the superior stock and simmer for about 30 minutes until the fungus is softened. If still too crunchy, simmer for a further 15-20 minutes. Season to taste.

Tips

Choose the yellowish, dry snow fungus which is sold in clumps. Ready-soaked snow fungus becomes soft and mushy on simmering.

Snow fungus can also be added to stir-fried vegetables such as snow peas and bell peppers. For this, you may use snow fungus that is thinner and lower quality, but first simmer it for an hour before stir-frying.

TOP SHELL SOUP
HIONG LOR TONG

- 100 g dried top shell meat, washed and soaked for an hour
- ½ dried squid
- 3 chicken breasts with bone
- salt and pepper

Simmer the top shell meat till it is soft enough to bite into, about 30 minutes or longer.

Cut the dried squid into 2cm pieces and wash them thoroughly.

Transfer the top shell and simmering water, and the squid pieces into a large pot with the chicken breasts. Add water to cover the ingredients and bring to boil. Simmer for 1-2 hours. Season to taste.

Tips

Dried squid (jiong yu) are about 20-25cm long with short tentacles. Do not mistake them for octopus (muck yu) which has long tentacles.

99/
BIRD'S NEST CHICKEN SOUP
YEEN WOR DUN GYE

If there is one dish I miss most, it is this. Mother would painstakingly clean the nests of every bit of feather and dirt using a pair of tweezers and soak them for hours. Truth be told, bird's nest have almost no taste to speak of, but they have a glorious mouth-feel that is smooth yet with a light bite.

- 1 chicken, about 1½-2 kg
- 7-8 bird's nests, soaked and cleaned
- salt and pepper

Bone the chicken starting from the opening of the body cavity. Cut the joints where the thigh bones and wing drumlets meet the body. Be careful not to break the skin.

Shred the bird's nests into threads.

Rub the chicken with salt, on the skin and in the cavity. Stuff the soaked and cleaned bird's nest into the cavity and sew up the opening.

Place the chicken into a double-boiler. Add water to cover the chicken and double-boil for 3 hours. Season the soup with salt and pepper.

Transfer into a soup tureen. To serve, use a big scoop to cut into the stuffed chicken and serve chunks of bird's nest and chicken meat in each bowl of soup.

Tips

An old chicken would give the soup a more intense flavour, but the meat would be tougher.

If boning the chicken is too much trouble, you may stuff the bird's nest into the body cavity, but you would have to dig the bird's nest out when serving.

If you can't be bothered to clean the bird's nests, you may buy the ready-cleaned ones sold in packets, although some may be fake, and it would be difficult to tell.

If you don't have a double-boiler, you may use a pot with a cover and steam it in a wok, topping up the water in the wok to prevent it from drying out.

ABALONE CHICKEN SOUP
BAU YU BO GYE

- 4 medium-sized dried abalones
- 3 chicken breasts with bone
- 10 dried scallops, soaked and shredded; keep the water
- salt and pepper

Soak the abalones over 2 days in the fridge to soften them, changing the water after the first day. Clean the dirt from around the frilly edges, brush the sides and the grooves with a small brush. Remove the small black knob near one end. Transfer into a pot and add enough water to cover the abalones. Simmer for 2 hours. Turn off the heat and keep the pot covered. When cool, keep the pot, abalone and water in the fridge overnight. Repeat this the next 2 days, adding a little water each time before simmering. By then, the abalones should be soft enough to stick a chopstick into the meat.

Place the chicken breasts, shredded scallops and the soaking water, cooked abalone and the liquid it has been simmered in, into a slow cooker. Add enough water to cover the ingredients. Turn the cooker on to the automatic setting and cook overnight. Adjust the taste with salt and pepper.

To serve, transfer the chicken onto a serving plate. Slice the abalones and place around the chicken. You may leave the shredded scallops in the soup or transfer them to the serving plate. Pour the soup into a soup tureen or ladle into individual soup bowls.

Tips

If the larger abalones are too costly, there are now tiny abalones on sale, about 1-2cm long. Nothing wrong with using these, except you will need about 20 or more for the soup.

I am not sure how Mother devised this method of braising the abalones to soften them, but it sure beats simmering and watching the pot and topping up with water for hours on end. Her pot of abalones would sit on the stove for days, simmering gently while she cooks the daily meals. Occasionally, when she is out of time, she would use a pressure cooker, but the texture of the precious seafood would not be the same.

P11/
BEANCURD STICK SOUP
FOO JOKE BARK GOR TONG

- 100 g beancurd sticks, soaked for 2 hours
- 200 g gingko nuts, shelled and peeled
- 2 chicken breasts with bone or 500g pork bones, blanched
- 4 dried scallops, soaked and shredded; keep the water
- salt and pepper

Cut the beancurd sticks into 10cm pieces.

Transfer the beancurd sticks into a large pot and fill it halfway with water. Bring to boil and simmer for 10 minutes. Add rest of the ingredients and simmer 1-1½ hours until the meat is tender and the beancurd sticks are soft. Season to taste.

Tip
Simmer the shelled gingko nuts for a minute with a dash of bicarbonate of soda to make the skin easier to peel.

CORDYCEPS SOUP
DOONG CHOONG CHOE BO GYE

There was a time when cordyceps were sold in square bundles tied with red string, costing as little as 20 cents a bundle; okay, so this was many decades ago. After dinner, my sister and I would fight over the worm-like strips, dipping each into soya sauce and biting off the "worm" part and discarding the black stem. We had no idea it was really a worm that had been invaded by fungus that took over the creature and turned it into part of a plant. We never dreamed how expensive they would become several decades later. Nor how cherished they would be for their health benefits.

- 20-30 cordyceps, cleaned and soaked for 15 minutes
- 5 pieces dioscorea
- 20-30 wolfberries
- 10 red dates, soaked and deseeded
- ¼ cup dried longan
- 3 chicken breasts with bone
- salt and pepper

Place the cordyceps and the soaking water with the other ingredients in a pot and pour enough water to cover the ingredients. Bring to boil and simmer over medium heat for about 3-4 hours. Season to taste.

To serve, drain the soup into a tureen and transfer the ingredients into a plate with soya sauce for dipping.

Tips

Top quality cordyceps cost hundreds of dollars for a small bunch, especially those from high altitudes and cold climates such as Tibet. Lower quality cordyceps may certainly be used in making the soup.

The number of wolfberries, dates and longan will determine the sweetness of the soup. The amounts may be adjusted to suit individual taste.

𝒫13/
LOTUS ROOT SOUP
LEEN NGAU TONG

This recipe is the same as that for old cucumber soup except for the lotus root which gives it a completely different taste and colour. It is a family favourite, especially the gossamer-thin threads in the sliced roots.

- ½ large dried squid
- 1 long lotus root, cleaned and thickly sliced
- 500 g pork bones, blanched
- 10 red dates, soaked and deseeded
- 2-3 slices Chinese Kam Wah ham, blanched and dried
- salt and pepper

Cut the dried squid into 2cm pieces and wash them thoroughly.

Place all the ingredients into a large pot and add enough water to cover. Bring to boil and simmer for 2-3 hours. Season to taste.

Remove all the ingredients to a serving plate and serve the soup in a tureen.

Tips

Buy lotus roots that are covered in mud which, according to Mother, have a softer texture when cooked than the clean ones. Rather than try and prove her wrong, I always play safe and buy muddy roots.

When cooked, the lotus root slices should be soft, not crunchy like cucumber. The best lotus roots have a powdery mouth-feel (meen) and are delicious dipped in soya sauce.

Dried squid (jiong yu) are about 20-25cm long with short tentacles. Do not mix them up with octopus (muck yu) which has long tentacles.

SALTED VEGETABLE SOUP
HARM CHOY TONG

- 2 pieces salted pickled mustard green, soaked for 15 minutes
- 2-3 preserved plums
- 500 g pork bones, blanched
- 2-3 tomatoes, quartered
- salt and pepper

Place all the ingredients in a large pot and add enough water to cover.

Bring to boil and simmer for 1½-2 hours. Season to taste.

Tips

Choose pork with soft bones which are crunchy and edible.

If the soup is too salty for your taste, you may soak the salted vegetable longer to remove even more salt, or use fewer preserved plums.

Variation

The pork bones may be replaced with half a duck cut into pieces.

P15/
THREE-COLOURED CARROT SOUP
SARM SEK LOR BARK TONG

In fact, only one of the three is a carrot. The other two are radishes – white and green. For unknown reason, radishes used in Chinese food are called carrots, as in carrot cakes, the hawker stall favourite.

- 2 large carrots, cut into chunks
- 1 green radish, cut into chunks
- 1 white radish, cut into chunks
- 2 sweet corn cobs, cut into thick slices
- 500 g pork bones or 2 chicken breasts with bone, blanched
- 6 dried scallops, soaked and shredded; keep the water
- 2-3 Chinese Kam Wah ham, blanched and diced
- salt and pepper

Put all the ingredients, including the soaking water, into a large pot. Add enough water to cover. Bring to boil and simmer for 2 hours. Season to taste.

Tips

Green radishes are similar to white radishes but with green skin. If not available, replace with white radish.

For extra taste, you may replace half the water with chicken stock.

Variations

These are endless, using different vegetables and pork bones. Some examples: carrots, tomatoes, corn and large onions; carrots, barley, large onions; hairy marrow; pumpkin and carrots.

OLD CUCUMBER SOUP
LOE WONG GUA TONG

This is not the same as the green cucumber but are much larger with a rough, reddish-brown skin. After cooking, the flesh is soft and easily scooped with a spoon, delicious when drizzled with a little soya sauce.

- ½ large dried squid
- 1 old cucumber, about 1kg, seeded and cut into large pieces with skin
- 10 red dates, soaked and deseeded
- 500 g pork bones, blanched
- salt and pepper

Cut the squid into 2cm pieces and wash them thoroughly.

Place all the ingredients in a large pot and add enough water to cover. Bring to boil and simmer for 2-3 hours.

To serve, transfer the ingredients into a serving plate and pour the soup into a tureen.

Tips

Dried squid (jiong yu) are about 20-25cm long with short tentacles. Do not mix them up with octopus (muck yu) which has long tentacles.

You may use a slow cooker at the automatic setting.

Variation

The old cucumber can be replaced by lotus root, which appears as a separate recipe on page 13 only because it is a family favourite and has a completely different taste and texture from old cucumber.

P17/
WATERCRESS SOUP
SYE YONG CHOY TONG

Mother used to double-boil this soup. Now, she uses the slow cooker instead, grateful for its convenience. If there is a difference in the result, we have not noticed.

- 500 g watercress
- 2 dried duck gizzards, quartered and soaked overnight
- 3 fresh duck gizzards
- 500 g pork bones, blanched
- 50 g sweet almonds, soaked and peeled
- salt and pepper

Cut off about 6cm from the ends of the watercress stalks and discard. Cut the stalks where the leaves begin, about 10-12cm and tie the stalks with twine into a bundle. Wash the bundle and the leaves thoroughly.

Clean the fresh gizzards by cutting open the pouches and washing off the sand and peeling off the yellow skin inside. Cut each gizzard into two and score the thick muscles, slicing about three-quarter ways but do not cut through.

Put all the ingredients, except the leaves and the bundle of stalks into a large pot. Add enough water to cover and bring to boil. Transfer to a double-boiler or slow cooker set at automatic. When the soup is simmering, add the stalks, cover and cook for 2 hours. Add the leaves and continue to cook for a further 30 minutes. Season to taste.

Discard the bundle of stalks. When serving, include some almonds and strands of leaves in each bowl.

Tips

Be sure to buy the watercress that has long stalks and roots, usually sold in large bundles, and not the small bundles of short-stalked variety.

The water must be boiling before adding the stalks and leaves or the soup would be bitter.

Sweet almonds, also known as apricot kernels, are not the same as the normal almonds used in baking.

If you have neither a double-boiler nor a slow cooker, you may cover the pot tightly and steam it in a wok, but be careful not to let the water in the wok dry up. Or just simmer over very low heat, tightly covered.

WINTER MELON SOUP
DONG GUA TONG

Guests are always impressed when the soup is served from inside the whole melon.

- 5-6 dried Chinese mushrooms, soaked an hour, stalks removed; keep the water
- 1 tbs oyster sauce
- 4 fresh duck gizzards
- 10 small dried scallops, soaked and shredded; keep the water
- 2-3 slices Chinese Kam Wah ham, blanched and finely diced
  - oil for frying
  - soya sauce
  - pepper
- 1 medium-sized winter melon
  - salt
- 2-3 cups chicken stock
- 5-6 water chestnuts, peeled and diced
- 1 chicken thigh with drumstick, boned and roughly diced

Simmer mushrooms and soaking water in a small saucepan. Add the oyster sauce and simmer until the liquid is almost all evaporated. Cool and dice.

Cut the gizzards open and wash away the sand inside. Peel off the yellow skin lining the inside. Finely dice the cleaned gizzards.

Transfer the scallops into a bowl and decant the water into another bowl, discarding any grit.

Heat some oil in a wok and fry the mushrooms, gizzard, diced ham and scallops with soya sauce and pepper to taste.

Slice off the top of the melon about 2cm deep and keep the cut-off piece as the cover. Scoop out and discard the seeds, taking care not to scoop the flesh. Rub the inside with a little salt.

Transfer the fried ingredients into the melon. Add the diced chicken, water chestnuts, scallops soaking water and chicken stock till 2cm from the rim and cover with the cut-off top.

Place the melon into a large bowl and steam for 2-3 hours. Serve the whole melon in the bowl with a large ladle.

Tips

Some restaurants cut the top in a zig-zag manner — very fancy but really, it's more trouble than it's worth.

When dishing out the soup and ingredients, include scoops of the melon flesh. Eventually the melon will puncture and the soup will leak into the tureen, so be sure you have a tureen that is deep enough to hold the soup.

Variation

A simpler method is to cut the melon into large chunks, cut off the skin and cook the chunks with the ingredients in a large pot.

PIG'S BRAINS SOUP
JU NOE TONG

This is supposed to nourish the brains, what else!

- 2 pig's brains, cleaned and stripped of the membrane
- 6-8 wolfberries
- 4-5 pieces dioscorea
- ¼ cup longan meat
- 1 chicken breast with bone
- 3 cups chicken stock
- 3-4 slices of ginger
- salt and pepper

Pour the stock into a double-boiler and bring it to a simmer.

Add all the ingredients and slowly lower the brains into the stock. Double-boil over medium heat for about an hour. Season to taste.

P21/
PIG'S STOMACH SOUP
JU TOE TONG

Mother hates making this because cleaning of the stomach is an unpleasant chore.

- 1 pig's stomach
- a handful of coarse salt
- 3-4 tbs starch
- 5-6 papaya leaves, crushed
- 5-6 dried scallops, soaked and shredded; keep the water
- 500 g pork bones, blanched
- 2 pieces salted pickled mustard green, soaked for 30 minutes
- 2 bricks beancurd, about 300g

Cut open the stomach and rinse thoroughly with water. Rub the inside and outside of the stomach vigorously with coarse salt, starch and crushed papaya leaves. Massage for 20-30 minutes, stopping intermittently. Rinse with fresh water. If it still smells, repeat the cleaning.

Place the stomach in a large pot of hot water and simmer for 15 minutes. Remove from the pot and discard the water. When cool, cut the stomach into 1cm x 4cm strips.

Place the strips of stomach into a pot half-filled with fresh water. Add the soaked scallops and soaking water, and the pork bones. Simmer for 2 hours. Add the soaked salted vegetable and simmer a further 30 minutes.

Five minutes before serving, cut the beancurd bricks into 2cm cubes and add them to the pot.

Tip

Do not use silken tofu as they will break into bits.

Variation

Soya sticks and gingko nuts may be included in the ingredients.

PIG'S LIVER SOUP
JU YUEN TONG

Before cholesterol became part of our vocabulary, liver soup was considered extremely nourishing and especially good for countering anaemia.

- 200 g pig's liver, thinly sliced
- ½ tsp sesame oil
- 1 tsp soya sauce
- salt and pepper
- 1 cm piece of ginger, cut into strips
- 3-4 cups boiling water

Marinate the liver slices with sesame oil, soya sauce, salt and sliced ginger for 10 minutes.

Transfer the liver and marinade into a pot and add 3-4 cups of boiling hot water. Stir over high heat for a minute to separate the slices to ensure even cooking. Remove the pot from the heat and keep it covered. Season with salt and pepper just before serving.

Tip

If the slices turn bloody when the soup cools a little, return to the stove and simmer for a minute but do not over-cook.

CREAM OF WINTER MELON SOUP
DONG GUA YONG

There is no cream in this soup, which is thickened by adding the mashed melon.

- 400 g winter melon, about a 3cm thick slice
- 1 chicken breast with bone
- 10-12 small dried scallops, soaked and shredded; keep the water water
- 3-4 water chestnuts, peeled and finely diced
- 1 chicken cube
- 2 tbs crab meat
- 1 egg
- 1 tbs starch dissolved in 2 tbs water

Cut the melon into large chunks and slice off the skin. Place the chunks, the chicken breast and soaked scallops and soaking water into a large pot. Add enough water to cover the ingredients, bring to boil and simmer for about 20 minutes, until the melon chunks are soft.

Transfer the melon into a large bowl and mash it, then press the pulp through a sieve.

Discard the scallops and chicken bone and strain the stock through a sieve into another pot. Add the chicken cube and crab meat and bring to a boil.

Beat the egg with some water and stir it into the boiling soup. Add the starch-mixture, stirring it into the boiling soup until the soup thickens slightly. Serve hot.

Actual size

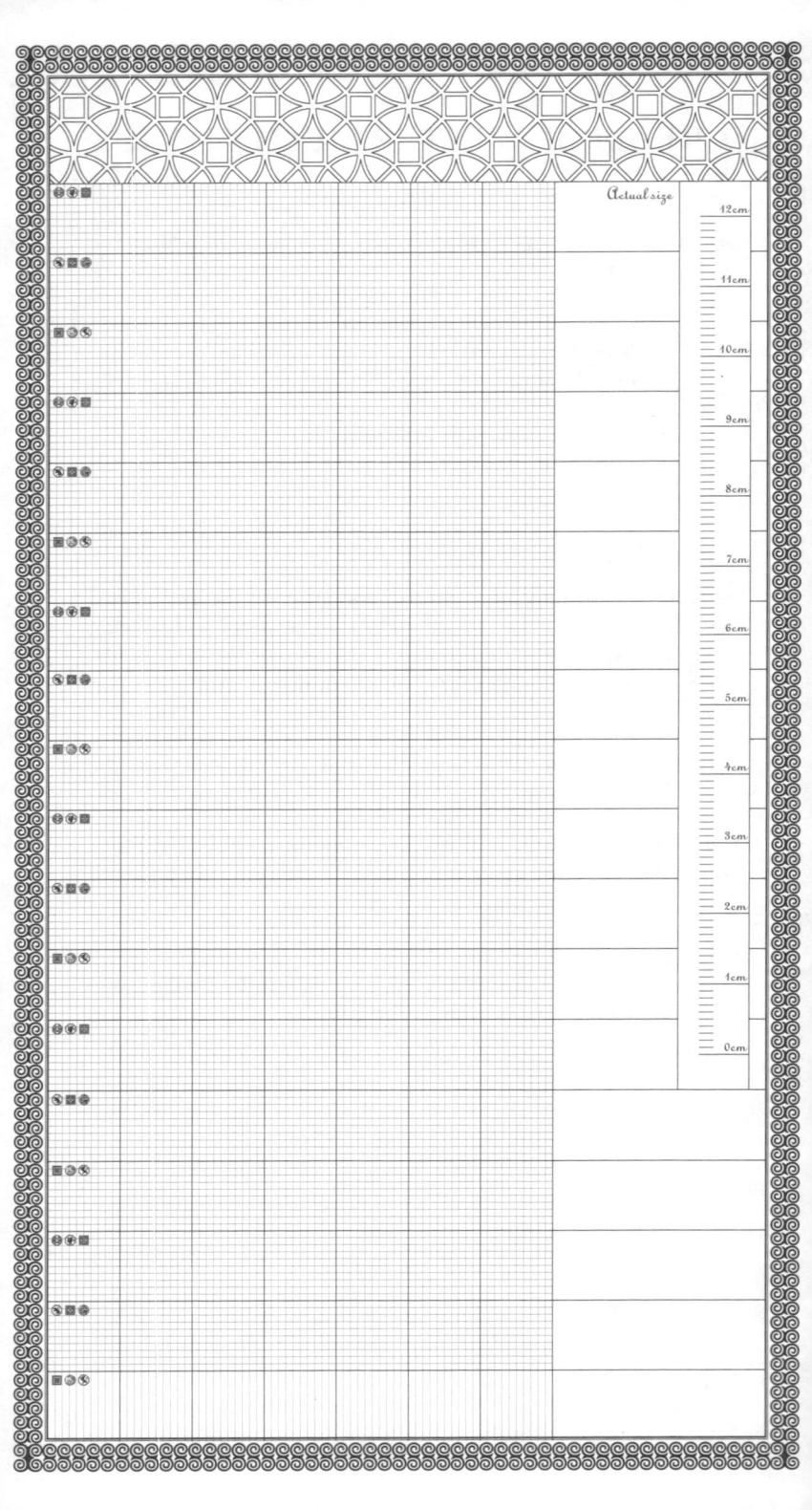

12cm
11cm
10cm
9cm
8cm
7cm
6cm
5cm
4cm
3cm
2cm
1cm
0cm

Poultry

WHITE CHOPPED CHICKEN
BARK JARM GYE

Unlike the white Hainanese chicken, this version does not have the garlic flavour or the oiliness. The meat should be tender, with a subtle sweetness. Only good quality oyster sauce, which is viscous and glossy, should be used for dipping.

> 1 chicken, about 1kg, with head attached
> salt and pepper
> oil for rubbing

Rub the inside of the chicken and the skin with salt and pepper. Tuck the legs into the body cavity and twist the wings to secure them on the back. Tie the chicken's neck with twine, with a loop strong enough to lift the chicken.

Fill a large pot with enough water to submerge the chicken. Add ½ tablespoon of salt. Bring the water to boil. Prepare another large pot filled with cold water.

Holding the twine, lower the chicken into the boiling water. When the water just begins to boil again, lift the chicken out of the water. Wait for the water to boil rapidly, then lower the chicken into the water a second time. When the water starts to boil again, remove the chicken. When the water is boiling rapidly, lower the chicken into the water a third time and wait for the water to simmer. Turn off the heat and cover the pot.

After an hour, remove chicken and lower it into the cold water in the other pot and leave it there for 30 minutes. Lift the chicken out and hang it up to drain the water. Rub the skin with a little cooking oil. When cooled, chop the chicken into pieces. Serve with the top quality oyster sauce.

Variations

Liver, gizzard and heart: If you like chicken liver and gizzard, they can be cooked in the pot together with the chicken. Clean the gizzard by cutting it open, washing off the sand inside and peeling off the yellow lining. Separate the lobes of the liver. Cut off the main vessels at the top of the heart and slit open the membrane around the heart and cut it open to wash off the blood inside.

Intestines: If you buy a live chicken and have it slaughtered, ask for the intestines. Use only the long narrow part of the intestines. Cut it open vertically with scissors. Use a sharp knife, scrape off the outer layer of fat and membrane and the inner lining. Rub generously with salt. Soak in salt and a couple of drops of alkaline water for 30 minutes. Wash thoroughly and soak in fresh water for another 30 minutes. When ready to eat, blanch in boiling hot water for about 10 seconds.

𝒫27/
CHICKEN IN DARK SOYA SAUCE
SEE YAU GYE

The cooking method is similar to white chopped chicken. The recipe leaves you with a lot of cooked dark sauce, which fortunately can be used for other dishes.

- 1 chicken, under 1kg
- 2-3 bottles of good quality dark soya sauce
- salt and pepper
- oil for rubbing

Choose a chicken with skin that is not torn. Wash thoroughly and drain. Rub the inside and the skin with salt and pepper. Tuck the legs into the body cavity and twist the wings to secure them on the back. Tie the chicken's neck with twine of about 6-8 cm loop strong enough to lift the chicken.

Pour the dark soya sauce into a pot with enough sauce to submerge the chicken. Bring to boil and lower the chicken into the sauce. When the sauce is simmering again, lift the chicken out. Turn the heat up and when the sauce is boiling again, lower the chicken in. Bring the sauce back to simmering and lift the chicken out.

When the sauce is boiling again, lower the chicken in for the third time and leave it in the pot. Turn up heat until the sauce is simmering. Then turn off the heat, cover the pot and leave the chicken inside for an hour.

Remove the chicken and hang it up to let the sauce drip. When the chicken has cooled, rub some oil on the skin and chop it into pieces and serve with some of the sauce in a bowl. The rest of the sauce can be used for cooking other dishes.

Tip

Good quality dark soya sauce is labelled "Top" or "Superior", the latter being the better one. They are thicker than the standard quality.

CRISPY SKIN CHICKEN
CHOOI PAE GYE

Some restaurants do such a good job of this because of the extreme high heat achieved with their huge burners, it is almost not worth the trouble of making it at home. But if you want a culinary challenge, this would be most satisfying when done well.

- 1 chicken about 1½kg, with head attached
- 1-2 tbs honey
- salt
- oil for deep-frying
- prawn crackers

Tie a piece of twine around the body of the chicken and under the wings and chop off the feet below the joint. Boil a big pot of water with the honey and reduce the heat to a simmer. Lower the chicken into the water and lift it up after 1-2 minutes.

Rub salt generously all over the chicken skin and in the cavity. Hang up the chicken for a couple of hours or more to air dry the skin. If the inside is still wet, dry with kitchen paper.

Heat a wok ¾ filled with oil over medium heat. When the oil is just beginning to smoke, lower the chicken carefully into the oil. Be sure the oil is not so hot as to burn the skin before the meat is cooked through. If the oil is not deep enough to cover the chicken, ladle the hot oil over it. Turn the chicken during the frying to brown the skin evenly. Be careful not to let the chicken stick to the wok or the skin will tear. Fry for about 30 minutes.

Chop into pieces and serve with prawn crackers.

Tip

The feet should be chopped below the joint to prevent the skin from shrinking during frying and exposing the joint and leg bone.

BRAISED CHICKEN WITH POTATOES
SHUE JYE MUN GYE

- 2 chicken thighs with drumsticks
- 2 chicken wings with drumlets
- 1 tsp soya sauce
- 1 tsp dark soya sauce
- 1 tbs oyster sauce
- ½ tsp sesame oil
- ¼ tsp sugar
- salt and pepper
- 3-4 waxy potatoes
- oil for frying
- 1 cup water
- 1 tbs starch mixed with 2 tbs water

Chop the chicken parts into pieces and marinate with soya sauce, dark soya sauce, oyster sauce, sesame oil, sugar, salt and pepper for an hour or longer.

Peel the potatoes and cut into 2cm chunks. Heat some oil in a wok and stir-fry the potatoes for a few minutes until the outside begins to brown.

Add the chicken pieces, the marinade and water to the wok. Cover and simmer about 30 minutes, tossing occasionally, until the chicken and potatoes are cooked. Be careful not to break the potato chunks.

To make the sauce, turn up the heat and add the starch-mixture a little at a time until the sauce thickens.

Tips
Frying the potato chunks first create a harder outer layer to prevent them from breaking during the cooking. Russet potatoes are not suitable for this dish as they become very soft and break easily when cooked.

Variation
Instead of the chicken parts, you may use half a chicken cut into 4-6 pieces.

P30/Poultry
BRAISED CHICKEN FEET
MUN GYE GEOK

- 6-8 chicken feet
- 1 tbs soya sauce
- 1 tsp dark soya sauce
- oil for frying
- 10 Chinese mushrooms, soaked; keep the water
- 1 tbs oyster sauce
- 1 tsp sugar
- 1 tbs brandy or Chinese cooking wine
- ½ tsp sesame oil
- salt and pepper
- 1 tbs starch mixed with 2 tbs water
- 200 g Chinese spinach

P3.1/

Clean the feet and peel off the tough yellow skin. Chop off and discard the tips of the claws. Marinate them with soya sauce and dark soya sauce.

Heat some oil in the wok and stir-fry the mushrooms with the oyster sauce, sugar, brandy and sesame oil for a minute. Add the mushroom soaking water and reduce the heat to a simmer. When the mushrooms are half-cooked, about 15 minutes, add the feet. Simmer until the feet are very soft. If the sauce in the wok is about to dry up, add 1 or 2 tablespoons of water.

With the sauce simmering, stir the starch-mixture into the wok a little at a time, stirring until the sauce thickens. There should be just enough sauce to coat the ingredients. Season to taste.

Cut the spinach stalks in 2 and rinse well, changing the water at least a couple of times. Boil a pot of water with 1 heaped teaspoon of salt and a few drops of oil. Blanch the spinach for a minute and drain.

Arrange the spinach on a serving plate and place the feet on top. Arrange the mushrooms on top of the feet with the stalk side down. Pour the sauce over the mushrooms.

Tips

As with other delicacies, Chinese mushrooms come in different qualities. The top of the caps with deep white cracks are known as "flower mushrooms" (far goo). The thicker, larger caps are generally better, but these also take longer to cook through.

The chicken feet should be so soft you can suck the individual bones clean.

Mother prefers starch to corn flour because it makes a clearer sauce. Also, with corn flour, the sauce becomes watery when cool.

Variations

You may replace the spinach with broccoli or lettuce.

With the broccoli, cut one head into florets and simmer them for 1-2 minutes. Arrange them along the edge of the serving plate.

With lettuce, break into individual leaves, use the large leaves to line the bottom of the serving plate with the curved edges of the leaves forming a bowl. Place the feet and mushrooms inside the leaves.

SALT BAKED CHICKEN
YEEM GOOK GYE

- 1 chicken about 1½kg
- oil for rubbing
- 1 cm piece of ginger
- 2-3 kg rock salt

Clean and dry the chicken and lightly rub the skin with oil. Cut the ginger into strips and rub the body cavity with the strips and leave them inside. Wrap the chicken in several layers of grease-proof paper or heavy-duty foil.

Fry the salt in a wok over medium heat till it is very hot, about 15 minutes. Transfer the salt into a large claypot. Make a depression in the salt and place the wrapped chicken in it. Cover the chicken completely with the fried salt.

Cover the claypot and cook over low heat for about an hour.

To serve, place the wrapped chicken on a serving plate and tear open at the table. Tear or cut pieces of meat from the carcass.

𝒫33/
SESAME CHICKEN
JEE MAH GYE

- 1 chicken about 1½kg
- 2 tbs oyster sauce
- 1 tbs soya sauce
- salt and pepper
- 1 tbs corn flour
- 3 tbs sesame oil
- 8 cm piece of ginger, cut into strips
- 1 tsp starch mixed with 2 tbs water
- 1 tsp toasted sesame seeds, optional

Cut the chicken into pieces. Season with salt, pepper, oyster sauce, soya sauce. Dust with corn flour.

Heat the sesame oil in a wok. Add the ginger strips and fry till fragrant.

Add the chicken pieces and seasoning, and stir-fry to mix thoroughly. Cover the wok briefly and continue to stir-fry till done. If the juices become dry, add just a little water.

Pour the starch-mixture into the wok, tossing it with the juices in the wok until the sauce thickens. Garnish with toasted sesame seeds.

P34/Poultry
CHICKEN AND HAM ROLL
FOR TOI GYE GUEN

When done well, this can look like a restaurant dish, with the meat in a ring around the red carrot, the green spring onions and the translucent cucumber.

- 4 chicken thighs plus drumsticks
- salt and pepper
- 4 sheets pig's caul
- 4 slices of ham
- 4 stalks spring onions, only green parts
- 1 carrot, peeled, cut into ½cm thick strips
- 1 cucumber, peeled, seeded and cut into ½cm thick strips
- 1 egg white
- starch for dusting
- oil for deep-frying
- 1 tbs starch mixed with 2 tbs water
- ½ cup chicken stock

Remove the bones from the thighs and drumsticks, making sure the thigh and drumstick meat is in one long piece. Season with salt and pepper. Bash the chicken pieces lightly with the blade of the chopper to flatten them and knock them gently with the blunt edge to prevent shrinking during frying. Remove the tendons. Season with salt and pepper.

Place a piece of chicken, skin side down, with the narrower end nearer you. Next to it, spread out a sheet of pig's caul.

Place a slice of ham on top of the thigh meat. Arrange a stalk of spring onion, a strip of carrot and a strip of cucumber in the middle horizontally on the ham, and trim them to the width of the meat.

Roll the chicken and ham tightly around the vegetable strips, using the skin to wrap the meat tight. Holding the roll firmly, place it on the caul. Fold the caul over, wrapping tightly around the chicken roll several times to form a fat sausage shape. Brush with egg white and dust generously with starch.

Deep-fry over medium heat until the caul is brown and crisp and the meat cooked through. Cool slightly and cut with a sharp knife into 1cm round slices.

Make a sauce by simmering the stock and stirring in the starch-mixture. Season with salt and pepper. Arrange the slices on a serving plate and pour the sauce over.

Tip

The caul is the thin fatty membrane that lines the pig's abdominal cavity. It looks like thin lace with fatty strips running across it. You may need to order it from your butcher. It comes in a clump that looks like pork lard. Open it slowly on a table to reveal the lace. Don't worry if it tears because you can roll over the tears and fold in the stray bits. When deep-fried, the fat melts, leaving a delicious crunchy shell.

CHICKEN WITH CLOUD-EAR FUNGUS
WUN YEE JENG GYE

- 2 cm piece of ginger, cut into strips
- ½ tbs brandy or Chinese cooking wine
- 8 small pieces cloud-ear fungus, soaked
- 1-2 dried Chinese mushrooms, soaked, cut into strips
- 5-6 red dates, soaked and deseeded
- 10-12 wolfberries, blanched
- ½ chicken cut into pieces or equivalent in thighs and wings
- 1 tsp soya sauce
- ½ tsp sugar
- 2 tsp oyster sauce
- ½ tsp sesame oil
- few drops of dark soya sauce
- salt and pepper

Mix the ginger strips with the brandy and squeeze the ginger to blend the juices with the brandy.

Place the soaked ingredients, wolfberries, ginger with the brandy, and chicken in a bowl. Add the soya sauce, sugar, oyster sauce, sesame oil, dark soya sauce, salt and pepper. Mix well and keep in fridge for 2-3 hours.

Arrange in a deep plate. When the chicken is at room temperature, steam for 20 minutes.

Variation

The dish may be fried. Here's how:

Marinate as above, leaving out the ginger and brandy.

Fry the ginger strips for a couple of minutes in a little oil, add some water and simmer to reduce a little. Mix a tablespoon of flour with 2 tablespoons water and stir into the wok to make a smooth sauce. Add the rest of ingredients and keep frying till chicken pieces are light brown.

𝒫37/
PAPER-WRAPPED CHICKEN
JEE BAU GYE

This used to be a party favourite, but has lost some favour in recent years. Pity, because the chicken has a distinctive fragrance. And none of the oil gets into the bag, so it is not as oily as other deep-fried dishes.

- 2 tbs starch mixed with water into a paste
- 4 chicken thighs with drumsticks
- 1 tbs sesame oil
- 1 tbs oyster sauce
- ½ tsp sugar
- 1 tbs brandy or Chinese cooking wine
- 1 tsp soya sauce
  salt and pepper
- 2 cm piece of ginger, sliced and cut into strips
- 4 spring onions, cut into 4cm pieces
  oil for deep-frying

Prepare a sheet of greaseproof paper and cut into 12 pieces, each 20cm by 20cm.

Fold each piece of paper in half and stick three sides down with starch to make a pouch.

Remove the bones from the chicken thighs and cut into 4cm pieces. Marinate with the sesame oil, oyster sauce, sugar, brandy, soya sauce, salt and pepper for an hour.

Insert a piece of chicken into each pouch together with a few strips of ginger and spring onions. Seal the opening with starch.

Deep-fry the pouches two or three at a time over medium-high heat for about 10 minutes. Scoop out the pouches with a slotted spoon and drain off the oil and transfer to a serving dish.

Serve and let diners tear them open over their rice to let the juices flow into the rice.

Variations

If you prefer not to deep-fry, you can bake the pouches at 375°C for about 30 minutes. But it won't have the same intense fragrance.

Theoretically, you could use fish, but somehow, Mother never did that.

CHICKEN WINGS IN PRAWN PASTE
HAR JEONG GYE

This is not a traditional home recipe. But with the availability of prawn paste in jars, the once restaurant-only item has become an easy dish for home dinners.

- 8 chicken wings with drumlets, cut at the joint
- 1 tbs prawn paste
- ½ tsp sugar
- 1 egg white
- starch for dusting
- oil for deep-frying

Marinate the chicken with the prawn paste and sugar for at least an hour.

Drain off the liquid. Lightly beat the egg white and coat the chicken with it. Dust with starch and leave aside until the flour is soaked with the paste.

Heat the oil and deep-fry the wings till golden brown.

Tips

The fried wings can never be as crispy as those from cooked-food stalls because a home kitchen cannot achieve the same high heat. Nevertheless, be sure the oil in the wok is on medium high heat so that the batter will cook quickly and not be soaked in oil.

There is a risk that the meat might not cook through by the time the batter is brown. To avoid this, cut the meat of the drumlets vertically down to the bone.

P39/
BRAISED DUCK WITH YAM
WOO TAO MUN NGARP

- 3 star anise
- 15 Szechuan pepper corns
- 3 tbs sugar
- 6 cups water plus extra
- ½ cup dark soya sauce
- salt
- 1 duck, about 2 kg, bishop's nose and neck removed
- 1 large yam, peeled

Put the star anise and pepper corns into a small muslin bag and tie it up.

Warm the sugar in a dry wok over low heat to melt it into a light brown liquid.

Carefully add 5½ cups water, dark soya sauce and salt and bring to simmer. Lower the duck into the liquid and put the muslin bag of spices into the sauce.

Cover the wok, leaving a small gap and simmer for 45 minutes to an hour, turning the duck occasionally. Test whether the duck is cooked by sticking a chopstick into the joint between the wing and the body. If the chopstick pierces the meat easily, the duck is cooked.

Remove the duck. Pour the sauce into a bowl and skim off the oil.

Pour half the sauce back into the wok and add ½ cup of water and bring it to a simmer.

Cut the yam into half vertically. Place the yam halves in the sauce and simmer over medium heat, turning the yam occasionally. Cook for about 30 minutes, until it is soft. Test by piercing with toothpick or chopsticks through the centre.

Remove the yam and cut into 1cm thick slices. Strain the sauce from the wok and add to remaining sauce.

Chop duck into pieces and arrange in a serving plate. Place the yam slices around it. Drizzle with sauce. Serve the remaining sauce in a bowl for dipping.

LOTUS DUCK
LEEN JEE NGARP

- 1 duck, about 2kg
- salt
- 1 cup oil plus extra for frying
- 200 g lotus seeds, soaked and peeled, centre shoots removed
- 200 g gingko nuts, shelled and peeled
- 10 dried Chinese mushrooms, soaked and diced
- 6-8 water chestnuts, peeled and diced
- 10 raw chestnuts, shelled and peeled
- 3 tbs dried prawns, cleaned, soaked and diced
- 6 salted egg yolks
- dark soya sauce for brushing

Seasoning for stuffing:
- ¼ tsp dark soya sauce
- ¼ tsp oyster sauce
- ½ tsp sesame oil
- ½ tsp sugar
- ½ tsp five-spice powder
- salt and pepper

Bone the duck by removing the skeleton in one piece, taking care not to break the skin, especially along the back. Cut the joints connecting the thighs to the body, and the wing drumlets to the body. Continue to skin the neck and cut the neck bone at the base of the head.

Cut off the webs and the gland near the bishop's nose. With a needle and thread, sew up the hole at the neck below the head. Rub inside and out with salt.

Heat some oil in a wok and stir-fry the lotus seeds, gingko nuts, diced mushrooms, water chestnuts, chestnuts and dried prawns with the stuffing seasoning until fragrant. Set aside to cool.

Stuff into duck together with the raw salted egg yolks, right into the neck. Do not pack tightly. Sew up the opening.

Heat a cup of oil in a wok. When it is just beginning to smoke, gently lower the duck into the oil and scoop the hot oil over skin. This firms up the skin a little. Remove from the oil and wipe the skin with kitchen towel. Brush lightly with dark soya sauce.

Put the duck into a deep dish and steam over medium heat for 3 hours. Be sure to top up the water in the steamer every 10-15 minutes to avoid it drying out. Scoop off some of the juice in the dish to prevent it from over flowing. To test for doneness, poke the shoulder joint with a chopstick.

Transfer the duck to a serving plate. Pour the juice into a saucepan and simmer for a few minutes. Skim off the oil and pour some sauce over the duck. Serve the duck with a large spoon with the remaining sauce on the side.

Tips

Scalding the duck with hot oil is a difficult manoeuvre, although it gives the skin a firmness which looks good. An alternative is to place the duck in the deep dish and pour boiling hot water over it before stuffing it.

To make the lotus seeds easier to peel, simmer them in water with a pinch of bicarbonate of soda for 2-3 minutes. They are also sold ready peeled, cleaned and dried, but they need to be soaked and remaining bits of the centre shoots must be removed.

Be sure to buy raw chestnuts as the dried ones, although ready peeled and more convenient, are not as sweet.

Simmer the shelled gingko nuts with a dash of bicarbonate of soda to make peeling the skin easier.

The duck bone may be used for making soup with salted vegetables and pork bones.

Shopping list

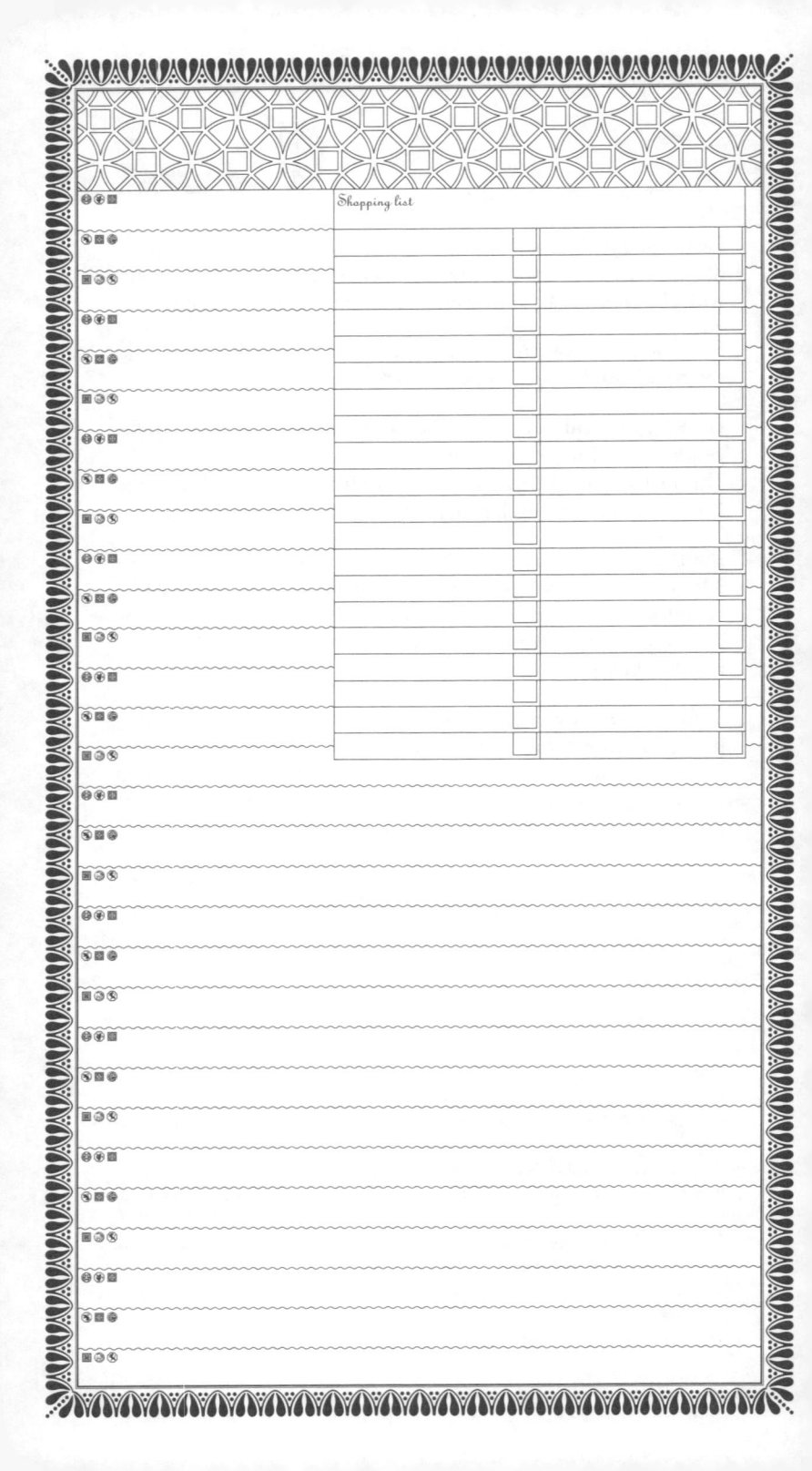

Guest list

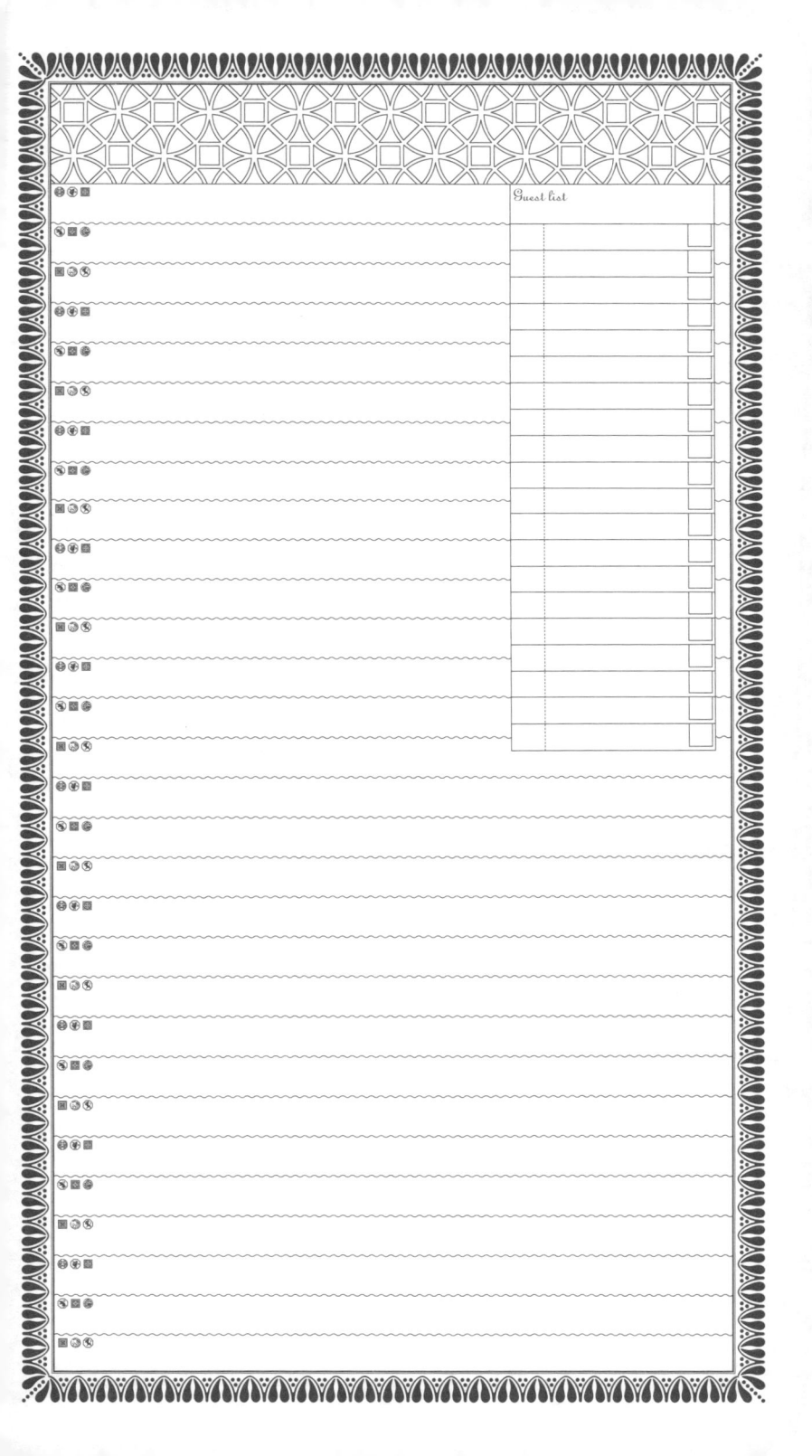

Actual size

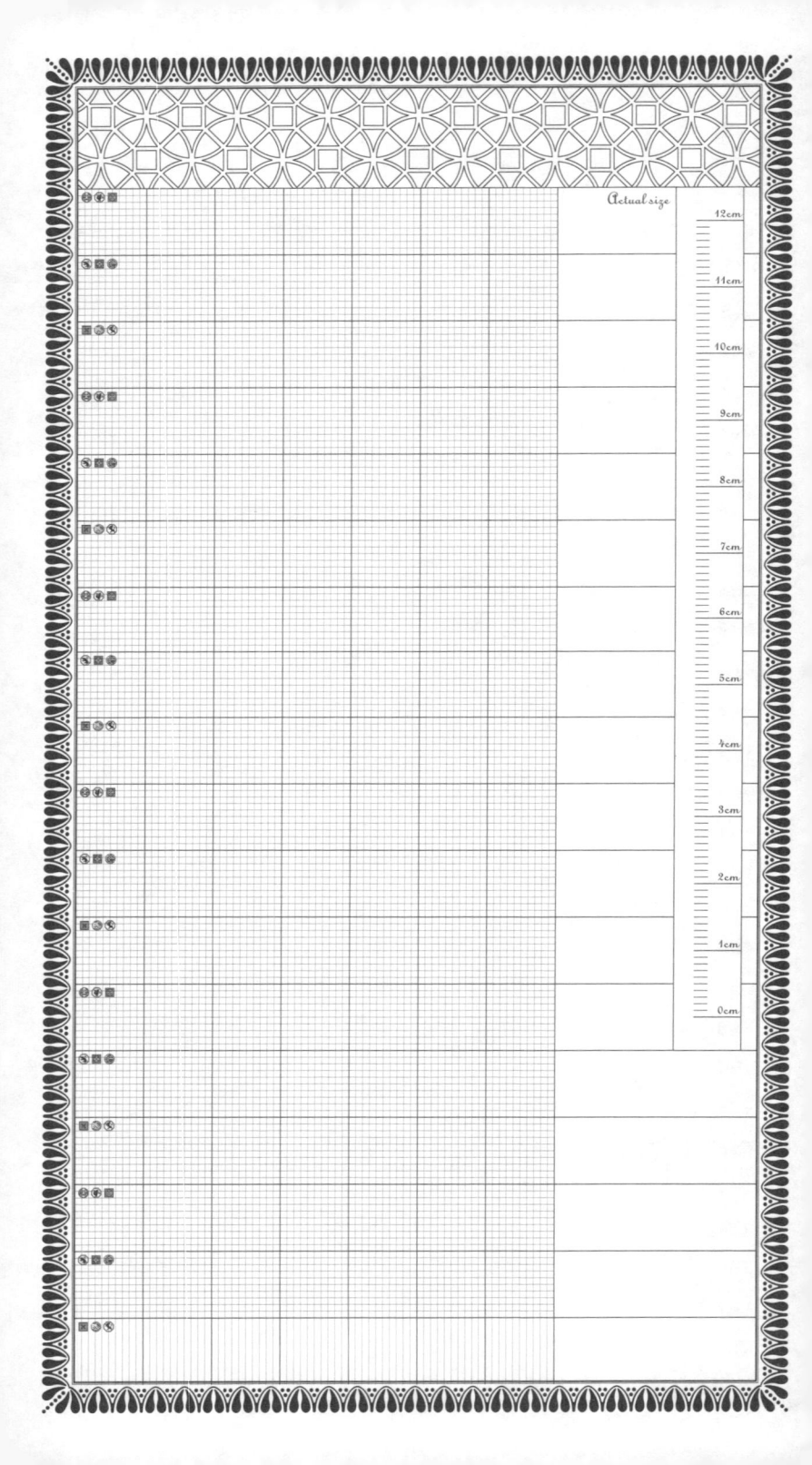

12cm
11cm
10cm
9cm
8cm
7cm
6cm
5cm
4cm
3cm
2cm
1cm
0cm

Pork

P46/Pork
MOTHER-IN-LAW EGGS
AH POR DARN *(for 8 eggs)*

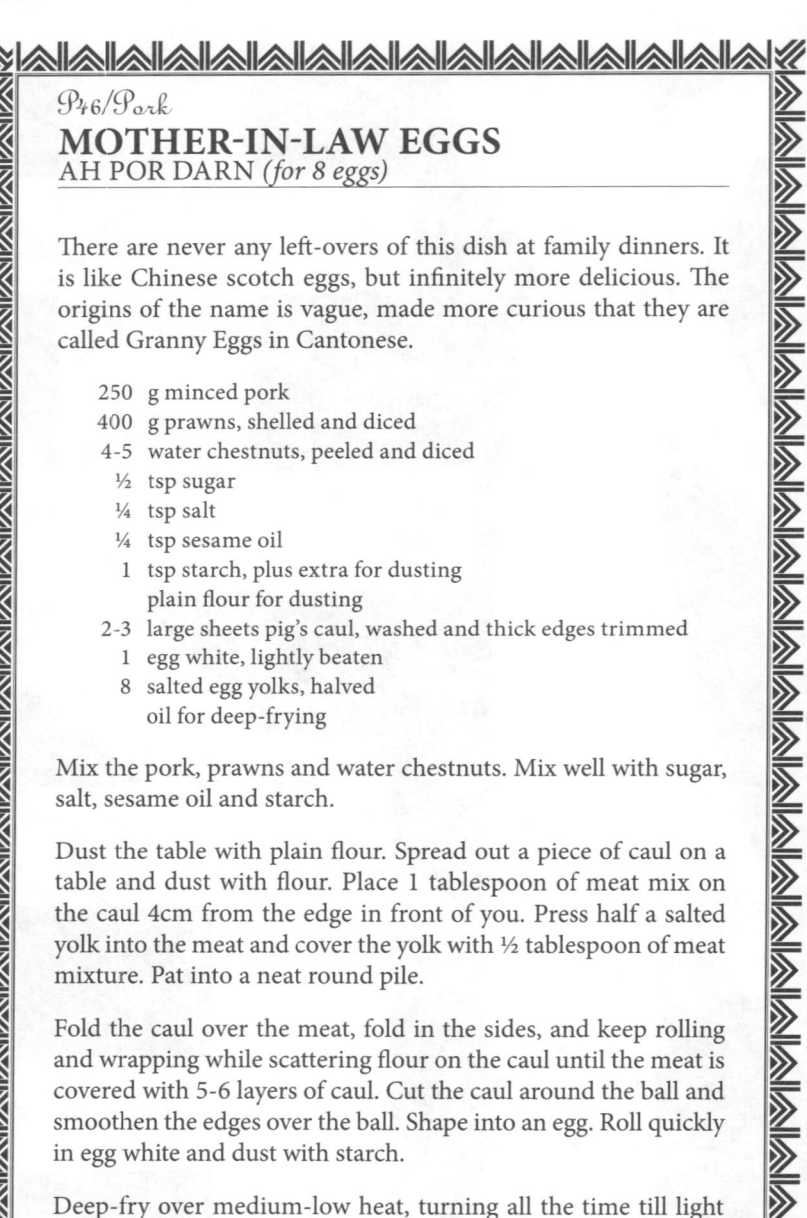

There are never any left-overs of this dish at family dinners. It is like Chinese scotch eggs, but infinitely more delicious. The origins of the name is vague, made more curious that they are called Granny Eggs in Cantonese.

- 250 g minced pork
- 400 g prawns, shelled and diced
- 4-5 water chestnuts, peeled and diced
- ½ tsp sugar
- ¼ tsp salt
- ¼ tsp sesame oil
- 1 tsp starch, plus extra for dusting
- plain flour for dusting
- 2-3 large sheets pig's caul, washed and thick edges trimmed
- 1 egg white, lightly beaten
- 8 salted egg yolks, halved
- oil for deep-frying

Mix the pork, prawns and water chestnuts. Mix well with sugar, salt, sesame oil and starch.

Dust the table with plain flour. Spread out a piece of caul on a table and dust with flour. Place 1 tablespoon of meat mix on the caul 4cm from the edge in front of you. Press half a salted yolk into the meat and cover the yolk with ½ tablespoon of meat mixture. Pat into a neat round pile.

Fold the caul over the meat, fold in the sides, and keep rolling and wrapping while scattering flour on the caul until the meat is covered with 5-6 layers of caul. Cut the caul around the ball and smoothen the edges over the ball. Shape into an egg. Roll quickly in egg white and dust with starch.

Deep-fry over medium-low heat, turning all the time till light brown. Just before serving, deep-fry again until golden brown. Cut vertically in half and serve immediately.

Tip

The caul is the thin fatty membrane that lines the pig's abdominal cavity. It looks like thin lace with fatty strips running across it. You may need to order it from your butcher. It comes in a clump that looks like pork lard. Open it slowly on a table to reveal the lace. Don't worry if it tears because you can roll over the tears and fold in the stray bits. When deep-fried, the fat melts, leaving a delicious crunchy layer.

HAKKA PORK BALLS
HAKKA LOU JU YOKE

A Hakka family who lived next door to mother's childhood home in Seremban used to make this. After frying the pork balls they would simmer them in a stew with vegetables and send some over as a neighbourly gesture. When mother's family adopted the recipe, they omitted the stewing and served the dish after deep-frying the pork balls. It has since become a family favourite.

600	g pork cut into 2cm chunks
3	tsp salt
7-8	tbs sugar
2	eggs
¼	tsp baking soda
5	tbs starch
6	tbs plain flour
	oil for frying
1	cucumber, cut into thin slices

Marinade the pork in 2½ teaspoons salt and the sugar overnight in the fridge. The next day, drain away the liquid.

Beat the eggs with ½ teaspoon salt and add it to pork with baking soda. Stir to mix well.

Add the starch and flour and mix thoroughly. The batter should be the consistency of pouring cream, just enough to coat a piece of pork when lifted from the bowl, but not so thick that there would be too much batter after frying. If it is too liquid, add a little more flour.

Heat about half a wok of oil over medium-low heat. Deep-fry a piece of pork till a light golden brown and taste it and adjust the seasoning of the batter accordingly. Fry 4 or 5 pieces at a time to a light brown colour, coating each piece with a thin layer of batter.

Just before serving, re-fry the pieces to a darker colour. Transfer into a plate surrounded by sliced cucumber and serve immediately.

Tip

The pork should have some fat and never all lean. Mother asks for the strip on the thin side of the rib rack but not all pork sellers will give her that. The alternative is to use belly pork without the skin.

P48/Pork
MINCED PORK STEAMED WITH SALTED FISH
HARM YU JENG JU YOKE

This is a humble home-cooked dish which was never on restaurants' menus until a few years ago.

- 3-4 Chinese mushrooms, soaked; keep the water
- 1 tsp oyster sauce
- 1 tsp soya sauce
- ½ tsp sesame oil
- pepper
- 200 g minced pork
- 2 water chestnuts, peeled and finely diced
- ¼ tsp starch in 2 tsp of water
- ¼ tsp sugar
- ½ tsp water
- salt
- tiny pinch of baking soda
- 2 cm piece of salted fish, washed and wiped
- 2 cm piece of ginger, cut into strips
- celery leaves to garnish
- oil for drizzling

Place the mushrooms into a small saucepan with the soaking water. Add the oyster sauce, ½ teaspoon of soya sauce, ¼ teaspoon of sesame oil and a dash of pepper and simmer until it is almost dry. Cool and dice finely.

Mix the minced pork, diced mushrooms and water chestnuts with the starch-mixture, the remaining sesame oil and soya sauce, water, salt and pepper, and baking soda. Spread and press into a deep dish.

Cut fish into small pieces and scatter on top of meat. Scatter ginger strips on top and drizzle with oil. Steam 10-15 minutes.

Serve in the deep dish garnished with celery leaves.

Tip

Mother says the best kind is mui hong salted fish from Kuantan.

Variation

The salted fish may be replaced with a salted egg. Mix the salted egg white with the meat and do not season with salt. Cut the yolk into pieces and scatter on top of the meat. Steam for 10-15 minutes.

P49/
PORK RIBS AND BITTER GOURD IN BLACK BEAN SAUCE
FOO GUA PYE GUAT

- 500 g pork ribs, cut into 2-3cm pieces and blanched
- 1 tbs black bean paste
- 5 cloves garlic, minced
- 1 tsp soya sauce
- 1 tsp dark soya sauce
- 1 tsp sugar
- oil for frying
- 1 clove garlic, smashed
- ¾ cup water
- 1 large bitter gourd, deseeded, sliced and blanched

Marinate the ribs with the black bean paste, minced garlic, soya sauce, dark soya sauce and sugar for at least an hour.

Heat some oil in a wok and fry the smashed garlic for a minute over medium heat. Add the ribs with all the marinade. Pour the water into the empty bowl to rinse it and pour the water into the wok. Bring to a low simmer. Cook covered until the meat is soft, about 30 minutes, stirring the ribs every 10 minutes. If the sauce starts to dry up, add some water and continue simmering. When the ribs are done, the sauce should be reduced to about ¼ cup.

If you have added too much water, remove the ribs and reduce the sauce. Add bitter gourd slices and simmer a further 5 minutes until the gourd slices are just done and not soft.

P50/Pork
PIG'S TROTTERS IN BLACK VINEGAR
JU GEOK BO HARK CHOE

Generations of Chinese postpartum women have eaten this, although some women and men have developed a liking for it at all times. For sure, it is an acquired taste.

- 500 g young ginger
- 1½-2 cups black vinegar, about 1 medium-sized bottle
- 1½-2 cups water
- 1 front trotter including part of the shoulder, cut into chunks and blanched
- 4-5 tbs sugar
- 1 tbs brown sugar or gula melaka
- salt
- 10 eggs, hard-boiled and shelled

Skin the ginger and smack lightly with the blade of a cleaver. Cut into 5cm pieces.

Pour the vinegar into a large pot and add the same amount in water. Add the ginger, pork, sugars and salt to taste. Bring to boil and simmer for an hour, until the pork is soft but not falling apart.

Turn off the heat. When completely cool, leave overnight in the fridge.

Next day, if the trotter pieces are not soft enough, simmer for a further 15-30 minutes. Adjust with salt and sugar to taste. Add hard-boiled eggs when warming up before serving.

Tips

If cooking for postpartum women, use old ginger.

Mother says that the Dog Brand black vinegar is best.

The dish tastes better when kept overnight, and is considered to be best on the third day. Unfortunately, the egg tends to become hard when kept this long. One way around it is to add enough eggs just for the day and simmer for 10 minutes before serving.

SWEET SOUR PORK
GOO LOU YOKE

- 500 g belly pork, skinned and cut into 1-2cm pieces
- 1 tsp salt
- 1 tsp sugar
- 1 egg, lightly beaten
- 1 tbs plain flour
- 2 tbs starch
- ¼ tsp baking powder
- salt and pepper
- oil for deep-frying
- lettuce leaves for serving

Sauce:
- 2 tbs tomato sauce
- dash of dark soya sauce
- 2 tbs sugar
- salt and pepper
- 1-2 tbs rice vinegar
- 1 tsp starch mixed with 2 tbs water

Marinate the pork with salt and sugar overnight or 4-5 hours in the fridge. Next day, pour away the liquid.

Add the egg, flour, starch, baking powder, salt and pepper to taste. Mix well. The batter should be creamy so that it clings to the meat in a thin layer. If it is too thin, add a little flour.

Deep-fry in medium heat, a few pieces at a time, turning in the oil to brown evenly.

To make the sauce, put all the ingredients except the starch-mixture into a wok and stir over medium heat until smooth. When simmering, add the starch-mixture a little at a time, stirring all the time until the mixture thickens.

Just before serving, bring the sauce to a simmer and add the fried pork pieces. Toss for a few seconds and turn off the heat, and stir to coat the meat. Serve immediately over a bed of lettuce.

CRISPY ROAST PORK
SIEW YOKE

Since Mother concocted this recipe not too long ago, we have stopped buying roast pork from the stalls.

- 1 kg belly pork in a single slab
- 1 tsp salt
- ½ tsp sugar
- ½ tsp five-spice powder

Wipe the skin dry. Insert two skewers diagonally into the meat in a cross to keep the slab flat when roasting.

Score the meat side half way into the meat 2cm apart. Rub salt, sugar and five-spice powder into the slits and meat.

Rub the skin with lots of salt. Pierce the skin all over with a sharp skewer. Leave aside for 4-5 hours or overnight.

Set the oven at 200°C and cook meat side up in a centre rack for 20 minutes. Flip over and bake for a further 20 minutes. Move the slab about if the skin is not browning evenly.

Change the oven setting to grill but leave meat at the centre rack. Watch the skin. When it starts to crackle, move it to a lower rack. When the skin has crackled evenly and just before it burns, remove from oven. When cool, chop into 2cm squares.

Tips

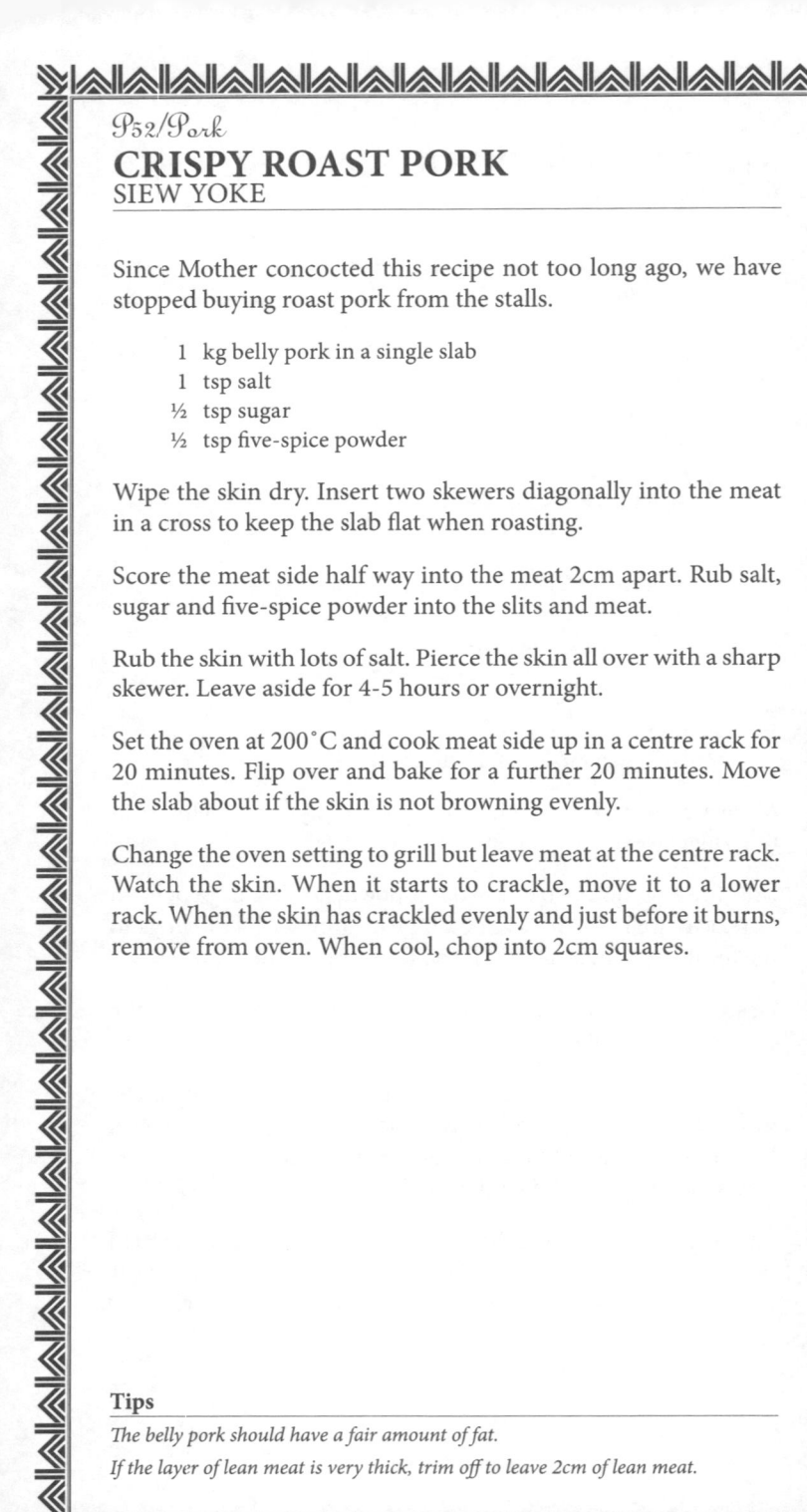

The belly pork should have a fair amount of fat.

If the layer of lean meat is very thick, trim off to leave 2cm of lean meat.

℘53/
ROAST PORK RIBS
SIEW PYE GUAT

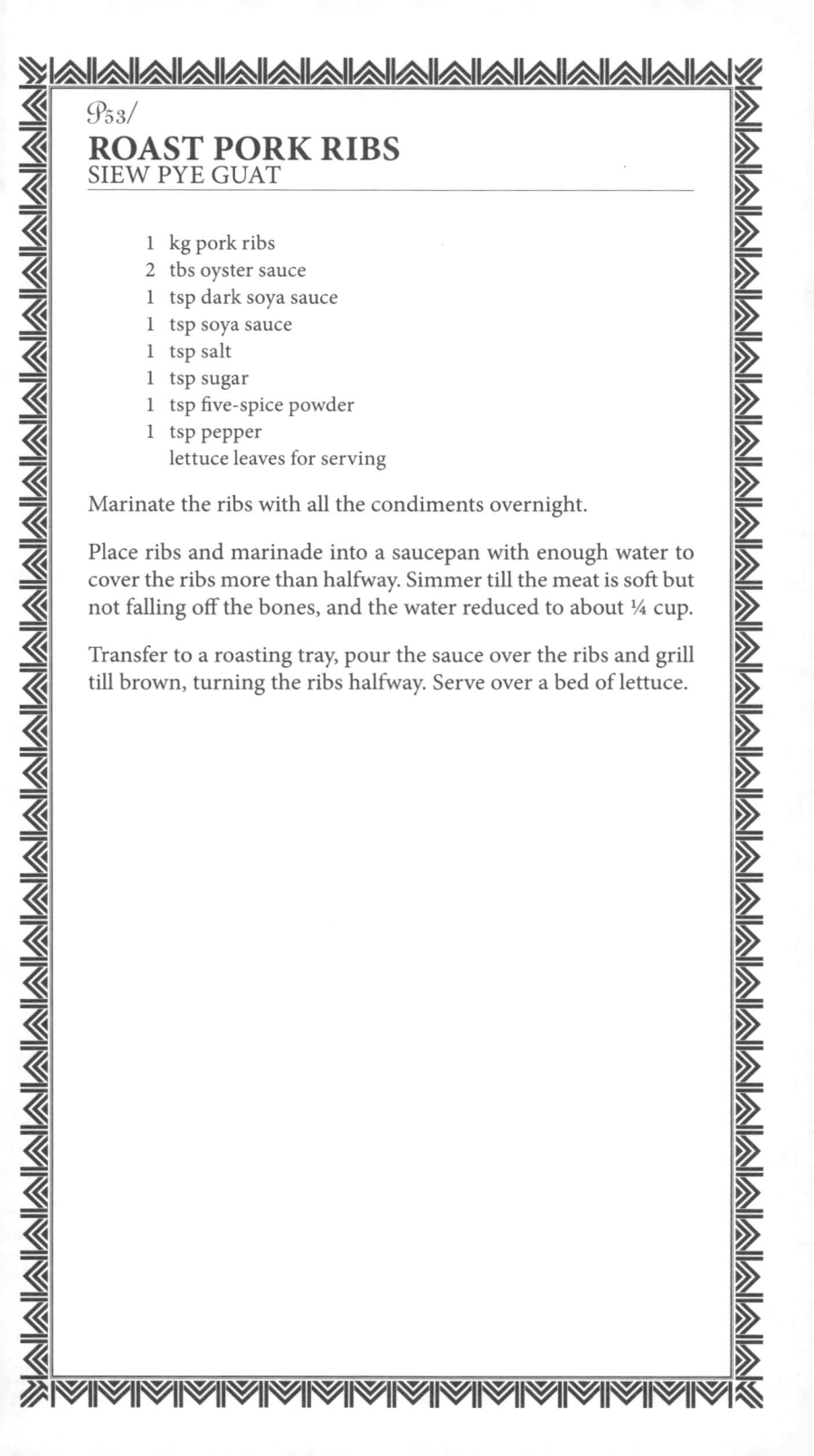

- 1 kg pork ribs
- 2 tbs oyster sauce
- 1 tsp dark soya sauce
- 1 tsp soya sauce
- 1 tsp salt
- 1 tsp sugar
- 1 tsp five-spice powder
- 1 tsp pepper
- lettuce leaves for serving

Marinate the ribs with all the condiments overnight.

Place ribs and marinade into a saucepan with enough water to cover the ribs more than halfway. Simmer till the meat is soft but not falling off the bones, and the water reduced to about ¼ cup.

Transfer to a roasting tray, pour the sauce over the ribs and grill till brown, turning the ribs halfway. Serve over a bed of lettuce.

P54/Pork
FRIED PIG'S LIVER
JEEN JU YUEN

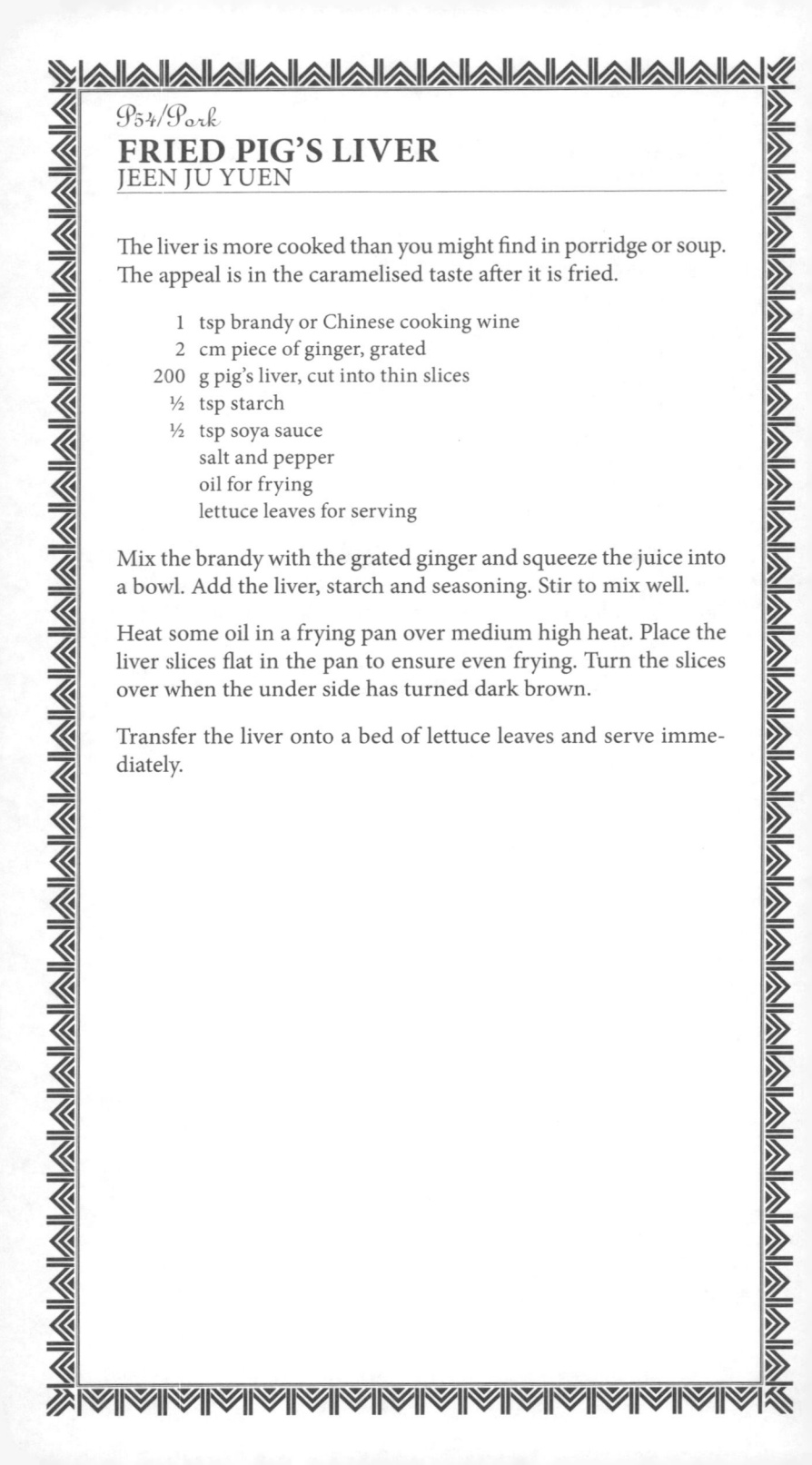

The liver is more cooked than you might find in porridge or soup. The appeal is in the caramelised taste after it is fried.

- 1 tsp brandy or Chinese cooking wine
- 2 cm piece of ginger, grated
- 200 g pig's liver, cut into thin slices
- ½ tsp starch
- ½ tsp soya sauce
- salt and pepper
- oil for frying
- lettuce leaves for serving

Mix the brandy with the grated ginger and squeeze the juice into a bowl. Add the liver, starch and seasoning. Stir to mix well.

Heat some oil in a frying pan over medium high heat. Place the liver slices flat in the pan to ensure even frying. Turn the slices over when the under side has turned dark brown.

Transfer the liver onto a bed of lettuce leaves and serve immediately.

P55/
PORK AND PRAWN DUMPLINGS
SHUI GAO

- 10 sheets of dumpling skin
- 100 g minced pork
- 200 g medium-sized prawns, diced
- 3 water chestnuts, peeled and diced
- 3-4 stalks of spring onions, chopped
- ¼ tsp sugar
- ¼ tsp chicken powder, optional
- ½ tsp sesame oil
- salt and pepper
- 1 egg

Make the egg noodles recipe (see page 108) but leave the dough in thin sheets. Cut them into rounds, 8cm in diameter to make dumpling skin.

To prepare the filling, mix all the other ingredients and stir so that it becomes a little sticky.

Place a teaspoon of the filling in the middle of a piece of skin. Wet the edges with a little water and fold it in half to make a semi-circle, pressing on the edges firmly together to make a good seal.

Bring a large pot of water to boil. Drop in 4 or 5 dumplings and stir while boiling to keep them from sticking together. When they float to the top, which takes about 2 minutes, they are done.

Serve with egg noodles or in a bowl of chicken stock as a soup.

Tip
The skin may be made in advance. After cutting to desired size, dust generously with starch before stacking them. Wrap in cling film and keep in the fridge for about two weeks.

Variation
The prawns may be kept whole and each dumpling should have one prawn.

To make wanton, omit the prawns. Cut the skin into 8cm squares. Place half a teaspoon of filling in the middle, wet the skin around the meat and scrunch up the skin around the meat. They may be boiled or deep-fried.

PORK BELLY IN DARK SOYA SAUCE
NG FAH LOH HARK SEE YEOW

- 2 cloves garlic, chopped
- oil for frying
- 2 strips of pork belly with skin, cut into 3cm pieces
- 3 tbs dark soya sauce
- 2 tsp light soya sauce
- 1 star anise
- 10 Szechuan peppercorns
- 1 tbs sugar
- 1 tsp salt
- ½ tsp chicken powder
- water

Fry garlic in oil in a saucepan over medium heat until light brown.

Add pork, dark and light soya sauce and fry for a minute.

Add the rest of the ingredients and enough water to cover the meat about halfway. Bring to boil and simmer for about an hour, stirring occasionally. When the skin is soft enough to cut with a spoon, it is done.

Tips

Use the best quality dark soya sauce you can find.
Long slow cooking over low heat will result in tender meat.

Shopping list

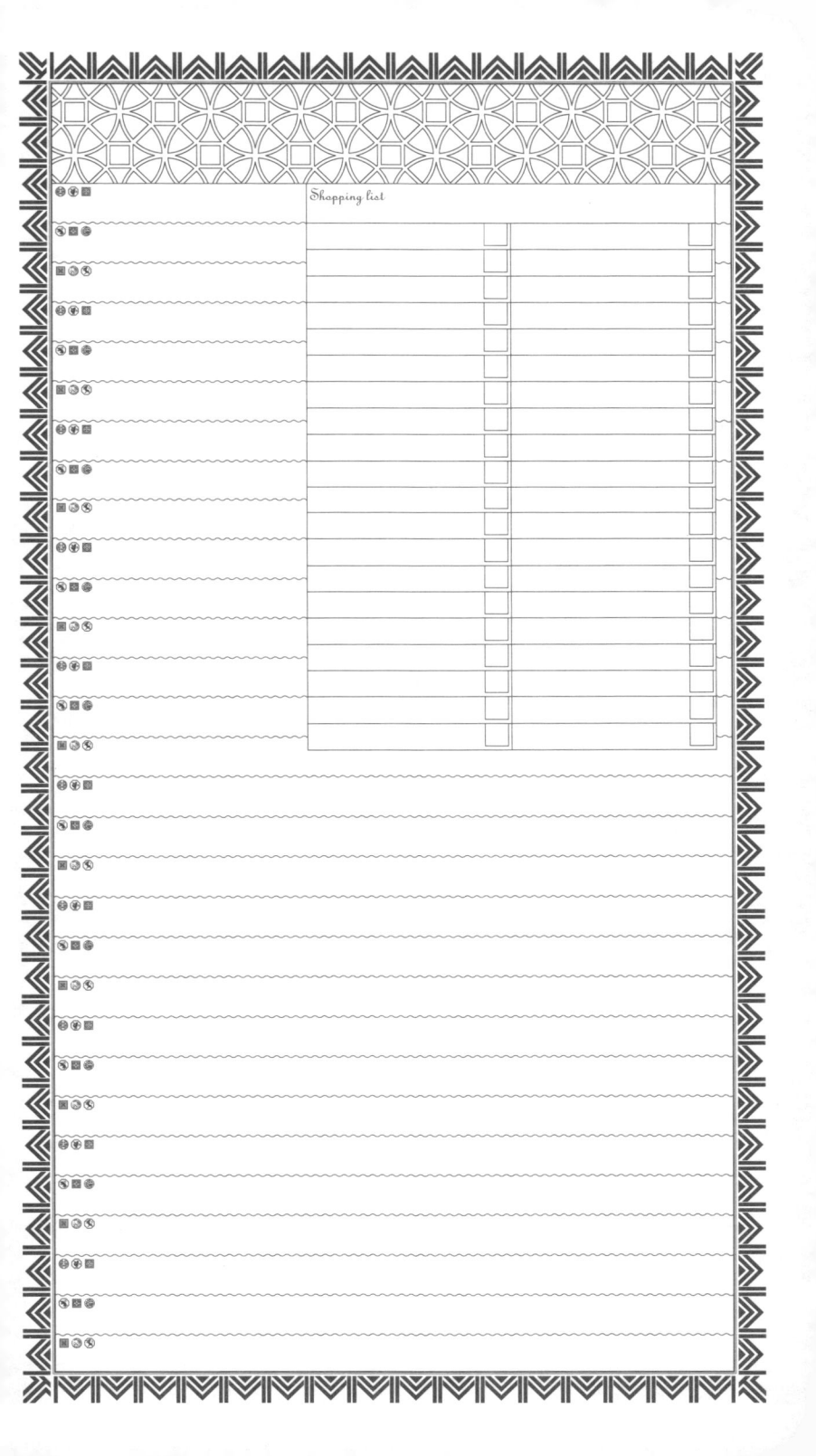

Guest list

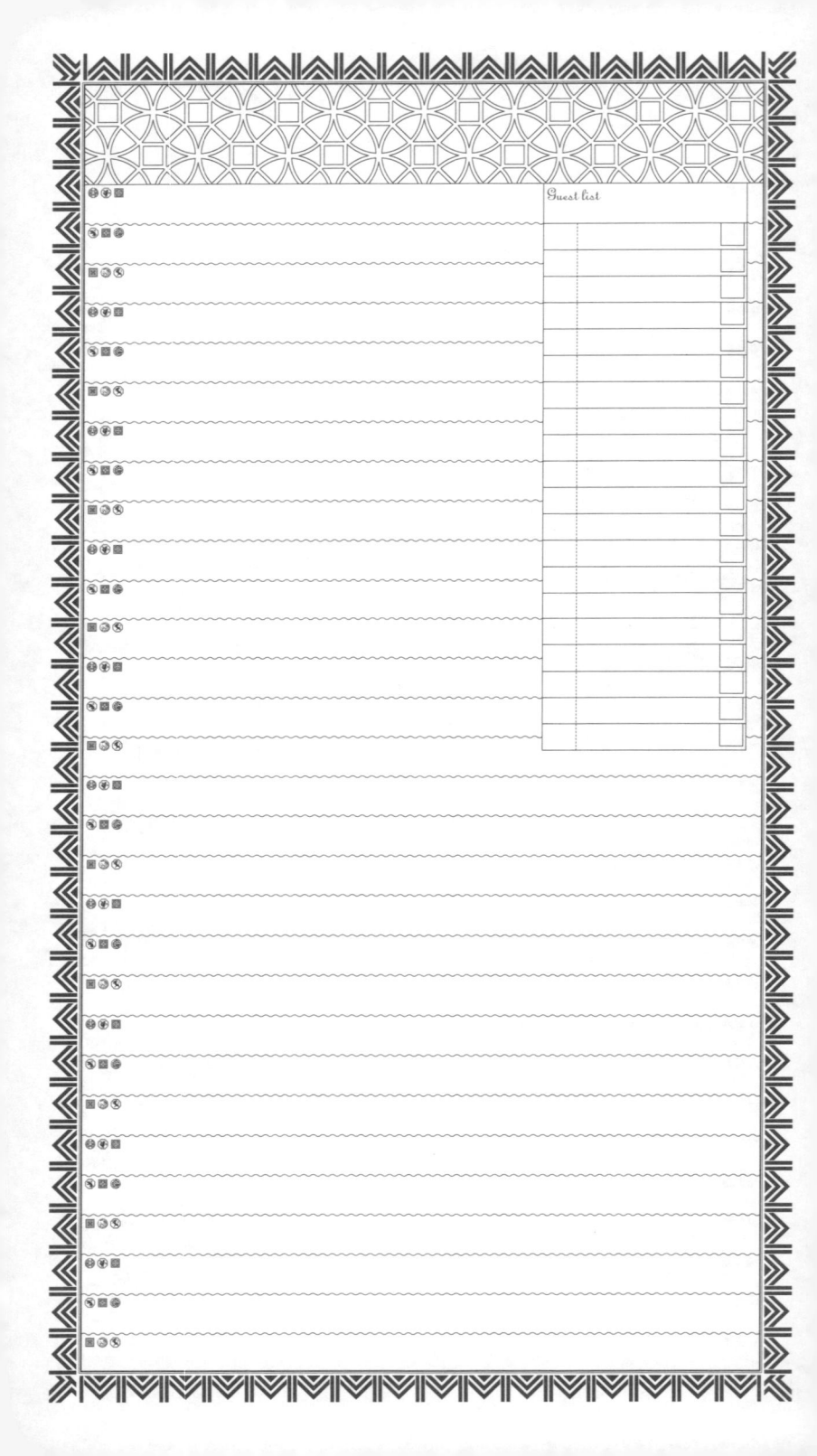

Seafood

STEAMED POMFRET
JENG CHONG YU

Silver pomfret is best for steaming. It is almost square, with grey scale patches on the body. The texture and taste of its meat, not to mention the price, is a world away from the more common white pomfret which is oval and pure white.

- 500 g pomfret, scaled and cleaned
- salt
- 3-4 slices of ginger, cut into strips
- 2 tbs cooking oil
- soya sauce
- sesame oil
- parsley, spring onions and chilli cut into 3cm strips to garnish

Rub salt on the fish, inside and out. Score the meat to the bone on either side. Place in a round plate. Drizzle with cooking oil and scatter the ginger strips over it.

Steam the fish in a wok or steamer for 6-7 minutes. To test if it is done, stick a chopstick into the thickest part of the body and it should go through easily.

Drizzle with soya sauce and sesame oil. Top with the garnish, and close the wok again for just a few seconds. Serve immediately.

Variation

You may replace the pomfret with cuts of black cod and threadfin (mah yau) or a whole garoupa. The body of the garoupa is thicker and the timing has to be adjusted accordingly.

P61/
FRIED GAROUPA
JEEN SEK BARN

    500 g red garoupa, scaled and cleaned
         salt
         starch for dusting
         oil for frying

Rub the fish inside and out with salt. Dust with starch. Make two cuts to the bone on each side of the body.

Heat 3 tablespoons oil in a wok over high heat. Slowly lower the fish into the oil and lower heat to medium. Do not move the fish. With the spatula, scoop the oil over the top of the fish.

After about 5 minutes, when the underside of the fish has browned to a crisp (check by lifting slightly with the spatula), turn fish over and fry other side for a few minutes. Test for doneness by sticking a chopstick into the thickest part of the body.

Drain on kitchen paper and place the fish in a serving plate.

Variations

To make a sauce to pour over the fried fish, mix 1 teaspoon soya sauce, 1 teaspoon oyster sauce, ¼ teaspoon salt, ¼ teaspoon sugar, 1cm piece of ginger grated, a dash of Chinese cooking wine and simmer with a mixture of 1 tablespoon starch and ⅓ cup stock or water to thicken.

You may fry a pomfret in the same way, using about 1 cup of oil so that it is almost deep-frying. The fins are crisp and can be eaten.

BATANG FISH STEAKS
JEEN GAU YU

This is a simple dish, but the salted fish flakes are sweet and smooth.

- 4 batang fish steaks
- 2 tsp salt
- oil for frying

Clean the steaks and dry with kitchen towel. Rub generously with salt and set aside for 30 minutes.

Heat some oil in a wok and fry the fish steaks over medium heat till golden brown on both sides.

P63/
FRIED TIGER PRAWNS
JEEN HAR LOKE

Only good quality prawns should be used for frying in the shell. Prawns are a must for Chinese New Year because the Cantonese word for prawns is *har* which sounds like laughter, and it is important to start the new year with laughter and happiness.

    300 g tiger prawns
         oil for frying
         salt
         lettuce leaves for serving

Trim off antennae of the prawns. Make a cut along the back and remove the intestine with a toothpick.

Heat 2 tablespoons oil and a pinch of salt in a wok over high heat. Add 4 to 5 prawns, placing them in one layer. When underside is red, about 2 minutes, turn the prawns over. Continue to fry the rest of the prawns.

Serve on a bed of lettuce.

Variations

If a sauce is desired, mix ½ cup tomato sauce with a pinch of salt and a pinch of sugar, simmer quickly in a saucepan and pour over the prawns.

For a more substantial topping, fry a chopped garlic with 1 large onion cut into quarters and 3 medium tomatoes cut into quarters. Add 1 cup tomato sauce and 2 stalks of spring onion cut into 2cm-long pieces. Stir-fry till the sauce begins to simmer. Thicken with a mixture of teaspoon starch and 2 tablespoons water, stirring over high heat. Add the fried prawns and toss for a minute.

PRAWNS WITH BELL PEPPERS
HAR CHOW DUNG LOONG JIU

- 500 g medium-sized prawns
- oil for frying
- 2 cloves garlic, roughly chopped
- 2 bell peppers of different colours, cut into eighths
- 5-6 baby corns, optional
- 1 large onion, quartered, optional
- 1 tsp oyster sauce
- 1 tsp brandy or Chinese cooking wine
- 1 tsp starch mixed with 2 tbs water
- soya sauce
- salt and pepper

Shell the prawns, leaving the tails attached. Slit along the back and remove the intestine.

Heat some oil in a wok and fry half the chopped garlic over medium heat for a minute. Add the prawns and fry till they are cooked and have turned red. Transfer to a plate.

Add some oil to the wok and fry the rest of the garlic, peppers, baby corn and onion for 2 minutes till the vegetables are cooked but still crunchy. Add the prawns and fry another minute. Transfer to a plate.

Stir the oyster sauce and rice wine into the starch-mixture. Pour into the wok over high heat and keep frying until the sauce thickens. Adjust to taste with soya sauce, salt and pepper. Add the prawns and vegetables and toss to mix well.

Variations

The prawns may be replaced with slices of any firm fish such as threadfin or cod.

Other vegetables may be used, such as broccoli, cauliflower, sweet peas, button and straw mushrooms and water chestnuts.

P65/
CUTTLEFISH WITH BROCCOLI
DIU PEEN CHOW GYE LARN FAR

- 1 large fresh cuttlefish
- 1 tsp oyster sauce
- soya sauce
- salt
- oil for frying
- 1 large onion, peeled and quartered
- 1 clove garlic, peeled and roughly chopped
- ¼ cup stock
- ½ tsp sesame oil
- 1 tsp starch mixed with 2 tbs water
- 1 head broccoli, cut into florets and blanched
- pepper

Split open the body of the cuttlefish and remove the head. Remove the insides and strip away the outer skin. Cut the body into squares and score the outer surface with diamond-shaped cuts. Season with soya sauce and salt.

Blanch the broccoli in salted boiling hot water and plunge into cold water to stop the cooking.

Heat some oil in a wok and fry the onion and garlic till fragrant. Add the cuttlefish and fry over high heat till the pieces are curled, about 30 seconds.

Mix the stock, oyster sauce, sesame oil with the starch-mixture. Over high heat, add it to the wok with the blanched broccoli and stir-fry till the sauce thickens. Adjust the taste with soya sauce, salt and pepper.

STEAMED CRABS
CHENG JENG HIE

- 3 live rock crabs
- 2 cm piece of ginger, cut into strips

Kill the crabs (see below) and pull off the body shells. Remove the gills and tails, and cut into two down the middle. Chop each half into two pieces, each piece with 3 legs.

Place the crab pieces in a large deep dish. Arrange the shells facing up. Scatter the ginger strips among the crab pieces.

Steam over high heat for 12 minutes.

Tip

The traditional, quick and painless (to the crabs) way is to stick a chopstick between the crab's eyes. If you are squeamish, put the live crabs in a plastic bag and put the bag into the freezer for an hour and a half. This knocks out the crabs, making them easier to cut into pieces.

Variation

If you use flower crabs, be sure to buy live ones. Once dead, they begin to deteriorate and the meat would have a mushy texture, despite the sweet taste.

R67/
FISH MAW STEW
MUN YU TOU

- 50 g fried fish maw, cut into pieces and soaked
- 2 cups chicken stock
- 1 egg
- ½ Chinese cabbage, chopped and blanched in salt water
- 6-8 fish balls, optional
- 6-8 meat balls, optional
- 6 quail's eggs, hard-boiled and shelled, optional
- 2 sea cucumbers, cooked, optional
- 1 tbs starch mixed with 2 tbs stock

Simmer the fish maw pieces in water for a few seconds. Drain and squeeze gently to remove most of the water. Transfer into a large pot with the stock and simmer over medium heat for about 15 minutes.

Beat the egg in a bowl together with 2 tablespoons of stock from the pot. Bring the stock and fish maw to boil and add the egg mixture while stirring.

Add the cabbage, fish balls, meat balls, sea cucumbers and quail's eggs and simmer for about 5 minutes.

Bring to boil and add the starch-mixture while stirring until the stock thickens slightly.

Tips

Fish maw is the swim bladder, sold in long puffed-up sticks. The large, round, golden yellow pieces are the most expensive, while the short thin sticks are the cheapest. Do not buy the wet version that is sold soaking in water as they disintegrate easily when cooked.

Sea cucumber takes ages to cook. See page 71. Cooked sea cucumber is sold in the market but the texture is not good as the sea cucumber becomes soggy easily. If you don't feel inclined to go through the hassle of cooking the sea cucumber, it is better to leave it out.

STUFFED CLAMS
YEONG HEEN

I have never had this anywhere outside of our home. It is delicious, but a real bother to open the clams.

- 500 g 3cm-wide clams
- ½ cup fish paste
- salt
- water
- ½ tsp starch
- oil for frying

Open the clams with a sharp tip of a knife and remove the meat. Rinse in clean water and remove the black bit in the meat. Chop finely. Wash the shells and set aside.

With a cleaver, chop the fish paste with a pinch of salt and a little water till the texture is firm. Add the clam meat and ½ teaspoon starch. Chop to incorporate into the fish paste. Transfer into a bowl and stir until the mixture becomes gummy.

Scoop a teaspoon of the mixture into a clam shell so that the filling forms a hump in the shell. Cover with another half shell and press the shells together firmly. When you run out of shells, roll teaspoons of the mixture into balls and flatten them slightly into patties.

Heat some oil in a wok. Fry the stuffed clams for 2 minutes over medium heat. Cover the wok for about 5 minutes or more to ensure they are cooked through. The shells should be lightly brown, and the patties without shells should be a golden brown.

ℛ69/
FISH SLICES WITH MUSTARD GREENS
YU PEEN CHOW CHOY SUM

- 300 g threadfin, cut into thick slices
- 2 tsp oyster sauce plus extra
- ½ tsp sesame oil plus extra
- 1 tsp soya sauce plus extra
- salt and pepper
- 100 g mustard greens
- 1 clove garlic, minced
- oil for frying
- sugar

Marinate the fish slices with 1 teaspoon oyster sauce, ¼ teaspoon sesame oil, 1 teaspoon soya sauce, salt and pepper.

Wash the vegetables and chop into 5cm sections.

Fry the garlic in some oil over medium heat for about 30 seconds. Add the fish and fry till the slices are half-cooked. Remove from the wok.

Heat another 2 tablespoons of oil and stir-fry the vegetables with a pinch of salt and a few grains of sugar, ½ teaspoon soya sauce, ¼ teaspoon sesame oil and 1 teaspoon oyster sauce. Stir-fry for a further minute or two.

Add the half-cooked fish and continue to fry until the fish is cooked.

Variations

Other firm fish may be used, such as cod, snapper and pomfret.

Other leafy greens may be used, such as Chinese baby broccoli, or baby Chinese cabbage.

FISH CAKE IN BEANCURD SKIN
YONG FOO PAE

- 2-3 sheets beancurd skin
- 100 g fish paste
- 1 tsp starch mixed with 2 tbs water
- oil for frying

Cut the beancurd skins into 10-12cm squares.

Mix the starch with water into a paste.

Place a teaspoon of fish paste in the middle and wrap the skin into a parcel, sealing with some starch-mixture.

Fry the parcels in a little oil over medium heat a few at a time for 1-2 minutes till the skin is light brown and the fish paste is cooked through.

Tip

It is too tedious to make fish paste from scratch. Buy it from the wet market.

971/
BRAISED SEA CUCUMBER
HOI SUM MUN GYE GEOK

Another premium dish that takes ages to cook but has such a fabulous mouth-feel.

- 3-4 medium-sized dried sea cucumber
- 6-8 dried Chinese mushrooms, soaked; keep the water
- 6-8 chicken feet
- 2 tbs oyster sauce
- ½ cup stock
- lettuce leaves for serving

Soak the sea cucumber for 4-5 days changing the water every day. After 2 days, when it is soft enough, cut open vertically and clean the inside. Continue to soak another 2 days, cleaning everyday. Remove the thin layer lining the inside.

Cut each sea cucumber into 2 or 3 pieces, depending on size. Simmer in a covered saucepan half filled with water for an hour and turn off heat, leaving the saucepan covered. When cool, simmer another hour and turn off heat, keeping the cover on. Do this over 2-3 days. The sea cucumber should be just under done. Test by biting a small piece; it should still be hard yet can be bitten through.

Simmer the mushrooms and chicken feet in oyster sauce, mushroom soaking water and stock for about 20-30 minutes, until the sauce has reduced to a thick glaze.

Add the sea cucumber and its juices and simmer a few minutes. Leave in the fridge overnight.

The next day, reheat and test the texture. If the sea cucumber is still too hard, continue to simmer till done. Serve over a bed of lettuce.

Tips

When sea cucumber is done right, it is soft and slightly gummy yet firm enough to be picked with chopsticks. If the piece breaks easily, it is overdone.

Dried sea cucumber is another seafood product that can cost a small fortune. The bigger they are, the more costly.

The ready softened sea cucumber sold in wet markets or supermarkets breaks up easily and lacks the firm, gummy mouth-feel.

P72/Seafood
ABALONE IN OYSTER SAUCE
HOE YAU MUN BAU YU

Whole, dried abalones are used here, not the canned variety. Because of their cost, they are likely to emerge mostly from affluent kitchens.

- 10 medium-sized abalones about 6cm long
- water
- oil for frying

Seasoning:
- 1½ cups superior stock
- 1 tbs oyster sauce
- ½ tsp sesame oil
- soya sauce
- pepper
- dark soya sauce
- 1 tsp starch mixed with 2 tbs stock
- 1 tsp brandy or Chinese cooking wine, optional
- lettuce leaves or Chinese spinach for serving

𝒫73/

Clean the abalones and soak in clean water for one or two days till slightly soft. Wash the dirt from the fringe and remove the knob from the top. Blanch for a minute and rinse.

In a saucepan half filled with water, simmer the abalones for an hour and turn off heat, leaving the abalones covered in the pan to cool. Repeat the simmering a couple of times during the day and keep overnight in the fridge. The next day, repeat the simmering two or three more times. Depending on the size of the abalone, you may need to simmer it for another day or so to soften them to the right texture.

Cut the abalones at a slant into ½cm thick slices and set aside.

Heat some oil in a wok over medium heat. Add the seasoning ingredients and simmer for a minute. Add the starch-mixture a few drops at a time, stirring after each addition. Stop adding when the sauce has thickened to a pouring-cream consistency.

Add the abalone slices and stir-fry to heat through. Add the brandy, do a quick stir and turn off heat. Arrange the abalone slices over a bed of lettuce or blanched spinach and pour the sauce over them.

Tip

When cooked, the abalone should be firm, yet easy to bite into. Press it with your finger and it should feel springy but not hard. Mother would start simmering the abalones three or four days before the dinner date. The saucepan would be kept on the stove in one corner and set to simmer whenever she was cooking the day's meals in the kitchen. This simmering would be repeated for another day or two. She says simmering for one long 4-5 hour period would not do the trick. It is the keeping of the abalones covered after each simmering that helps to soften the abalones.

Shopping list

Guest list

Actual size

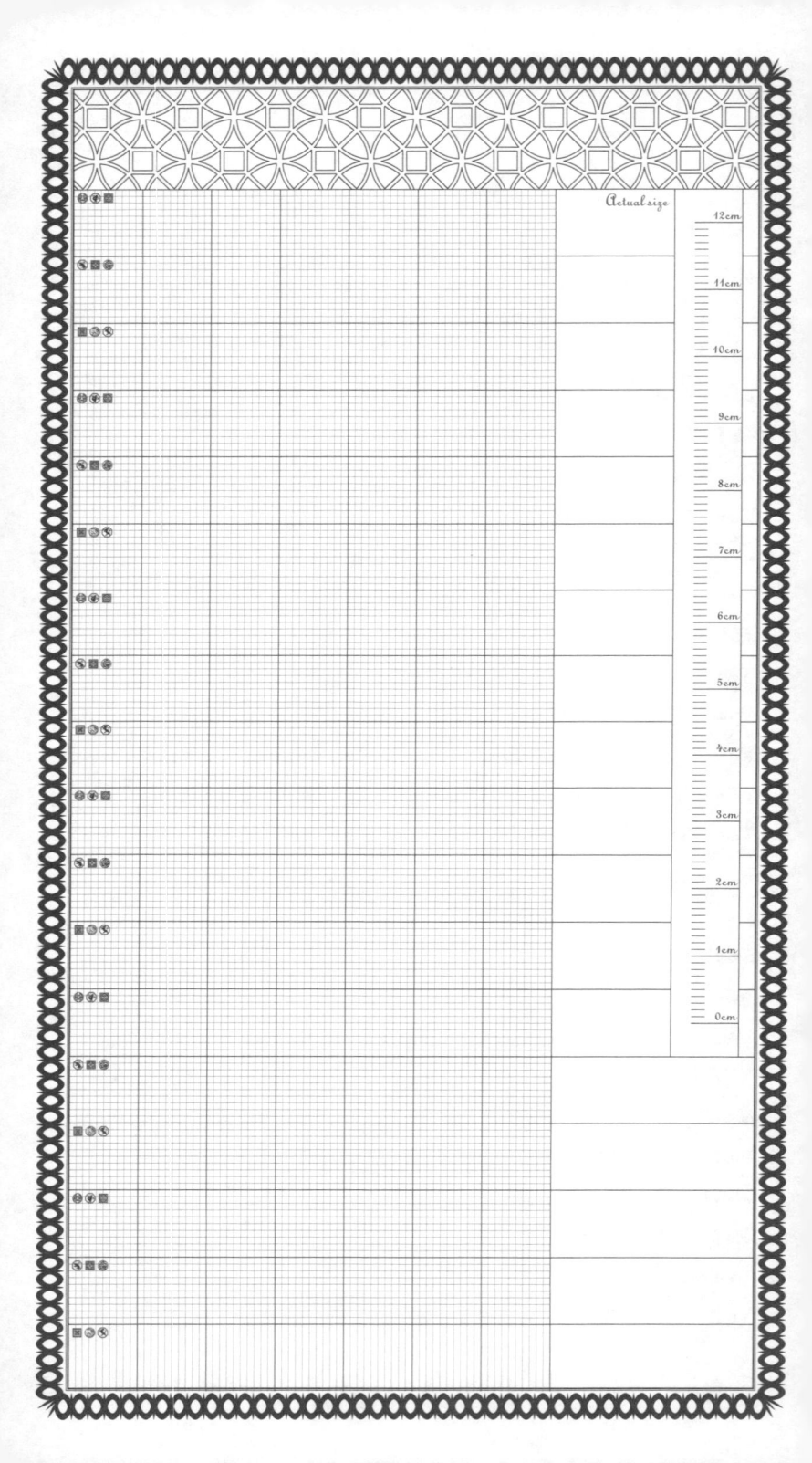

12cm
11cm
10cm
9cm
8cm
7cm
6cm
5cm
4cm
3cm
2cm
1cm
0cm

Vegetables

BOXTHORN IN SUPERIOR STOCK
GAU GAE SIONG TONG

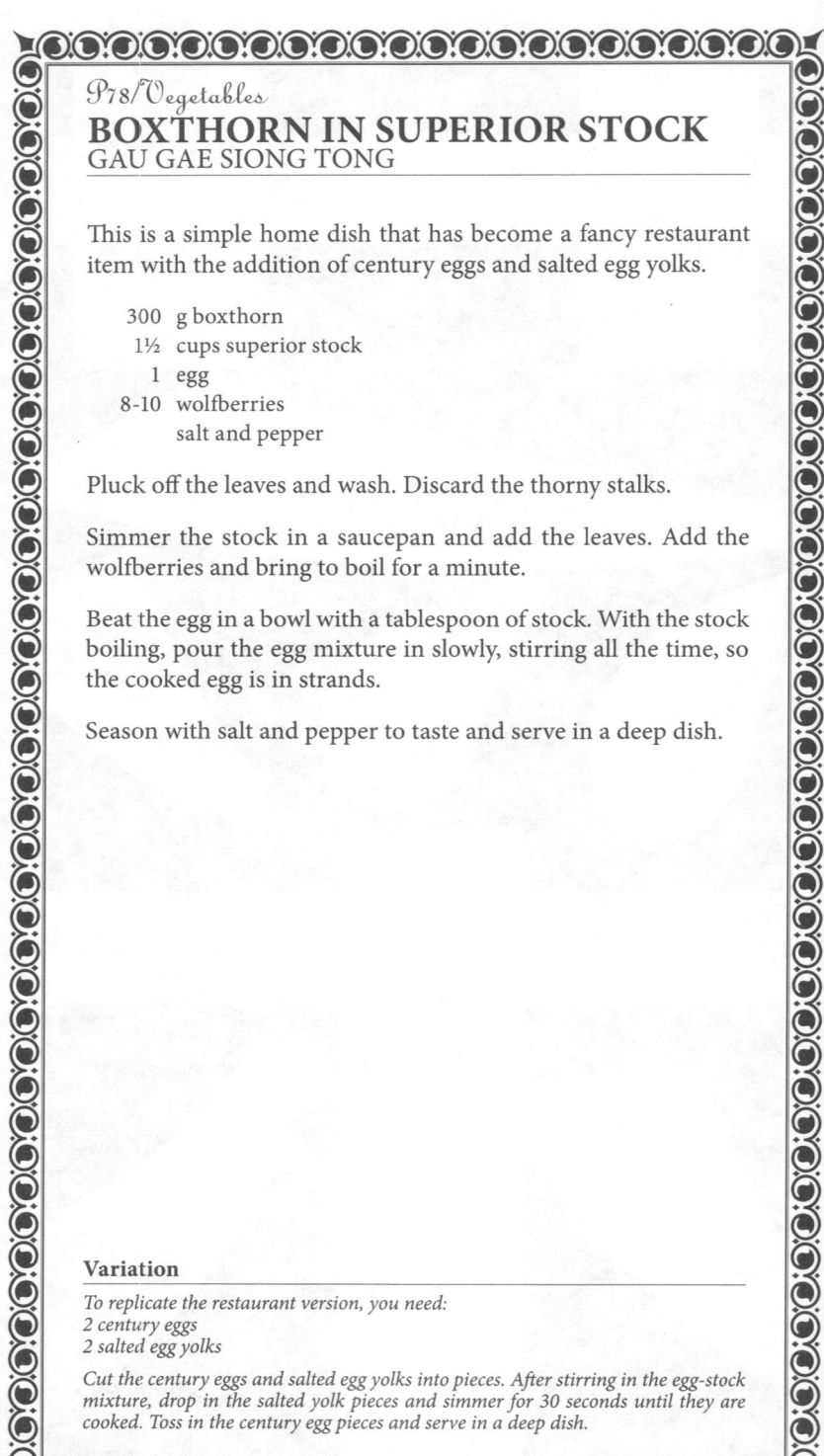

P78/Vegetables

This is a simple home dish that has become a fancy restaurant item with the addition of century eggs and salted egg yolks.

- 300 g boxthorn
- 1½ cups superior stock
- 1 egg
- 8-10 wolfberries
- salt and pepper

Pluck off the leaves and wash. Discard the thorny stalks.

Simmer the stock in a saucepan and add the leaves. Add the wolfberries and bring to boil for a minute.

Beat the egg in a bowl with a tablespoon of stock. With the stock boiling, pour the egg mixture in slowly, stirring all the time, so the cooked egg is in strands.

Season with salt and pepper to taste and serve in a deep dish.

Variation

To replicate the restaurant version, you need:
2 century eggs
2 salted egg yolks

Cut the century eggs and salted egg yolks into pieces. After stirring in the egg-stock mixture, drop in the salted yolk pieces and simmer for 30 seconds until they are cooked. Toss in the century egg pieces and serve in a deep dish.

HAIR SEAWEED WITH CLOUD-EAR FUNGUS
FATT CHOY WAN YEE

This is a must for Chinese New Year as the Cantonese name for hair seaweed sounds like the term for prosperity.

- 20 g hair seaweed
- water
- oil for frying
- 4-5 dried Chinese mushrooms, soaked and quartered; keep the water
- 2 tsp oyster sauce
- ¾ tsp sugar
- salt and pepper
- 10-15 lily bulbs, soaked
- 5 pieces cloud-ear fungus, soaked and blanched
- 5 pieces wood-ear fungus, soaked and blanched
- 10-15 lotus seeds, soaked and peeled, centres removed
- soya sauce
- 2-3 tbs chicken stock
- 1 tbs starch mixed with 2 tbs water

Wash the seaweed several times to rinse off the sand. Squeeze dry. Bring a pot of water to boil and add a little oil. Blanch the seaweed in the water. Drain and discard the water.

Transfer mushrooms and soaking water into a small pot and add 1 teaspoon oyster sauce, ¼ teaspoon sugar, salt and pepper. Simmer over medium low heat until very little liquid is left.

Simmer the lily bulbs in a small pot of water till they start to soften.

Heat some oil in a wok. Add all the ingredients followed by 1 teaspoon oyster sauce, ½ teaspoon sugar, salt, pepper, a drizzle of soya sauce and the chicken stock. Stir-fry and adjust the taste. Add the starch-mixture slowly while stirring over high heat until the sauce thickens.

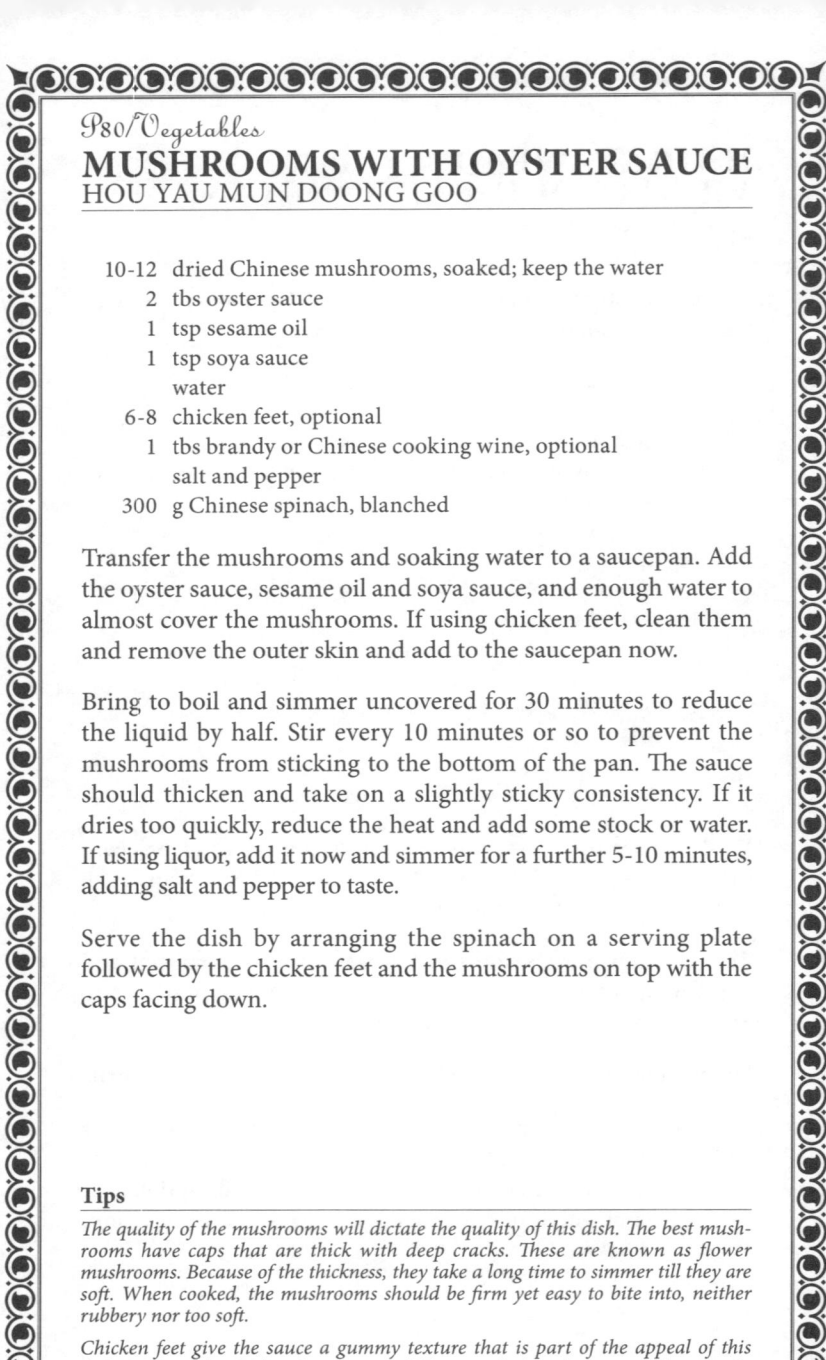

P80/Vegetables
MUSHROOMS WITH OYSTER SAUCE
HOU YAU MUN DOONG GOO

- 10-12 dried Chinese mushrooms, soaked; keep the water
- 2 tbs oyster sauce
- 1 tsp sesame oil
- 1 tsp soya sauce
- water
- 6-8 chicken feet, optional
- 1 tbs brandy or Chinese cooking wine, optional
- salt and pepper
- 300 g Chinese spinach, blanched

Transfer the mushrooms and soaking water to a saucepan. Add the oyster sauce, sesame oil and soya sauce, and enough water to almost cover the mushrooms. If using chicken feet, clean them and remove the outer skin and add to the saucepan now.

Bring to boil and simmer uncovered for 30 minutes to reduce the liquid by half. Stir every 10 minutes or so to prevent the mushrooms from sticking to the bottom of the pan. The sauce should thicken and take on a slightly sticky consistency. If it dries too quickly, reduce the heat and add some stock or water. If using liquor, add it now and simmer for a further 5-10 minutes, adding salt and pepper to taste.

Serve the dish by arranging the spinach on a serving plate followed by the chicken feet and the mushrooms on top with the caps facing down.

Tips
The quality of the mushrooms will dictate the quality of this dish. The best mushrooms have caps that are thick with deep cracks. These are known as flower mushrooms. Because of the thickness, they take a long time to simmer till they are soft. When cooked, the mushrooms should be firm yet easy to bite into, neither rubbery nor too soft.

Chicken feet give the sauce a gummy texture that is part of the appeal of this dish. Without the chicken feet, you would have to thicken the sauce with a starch-mixture.

Variation
You may replace the mushrooms with slices of canned abalone. Or have both.

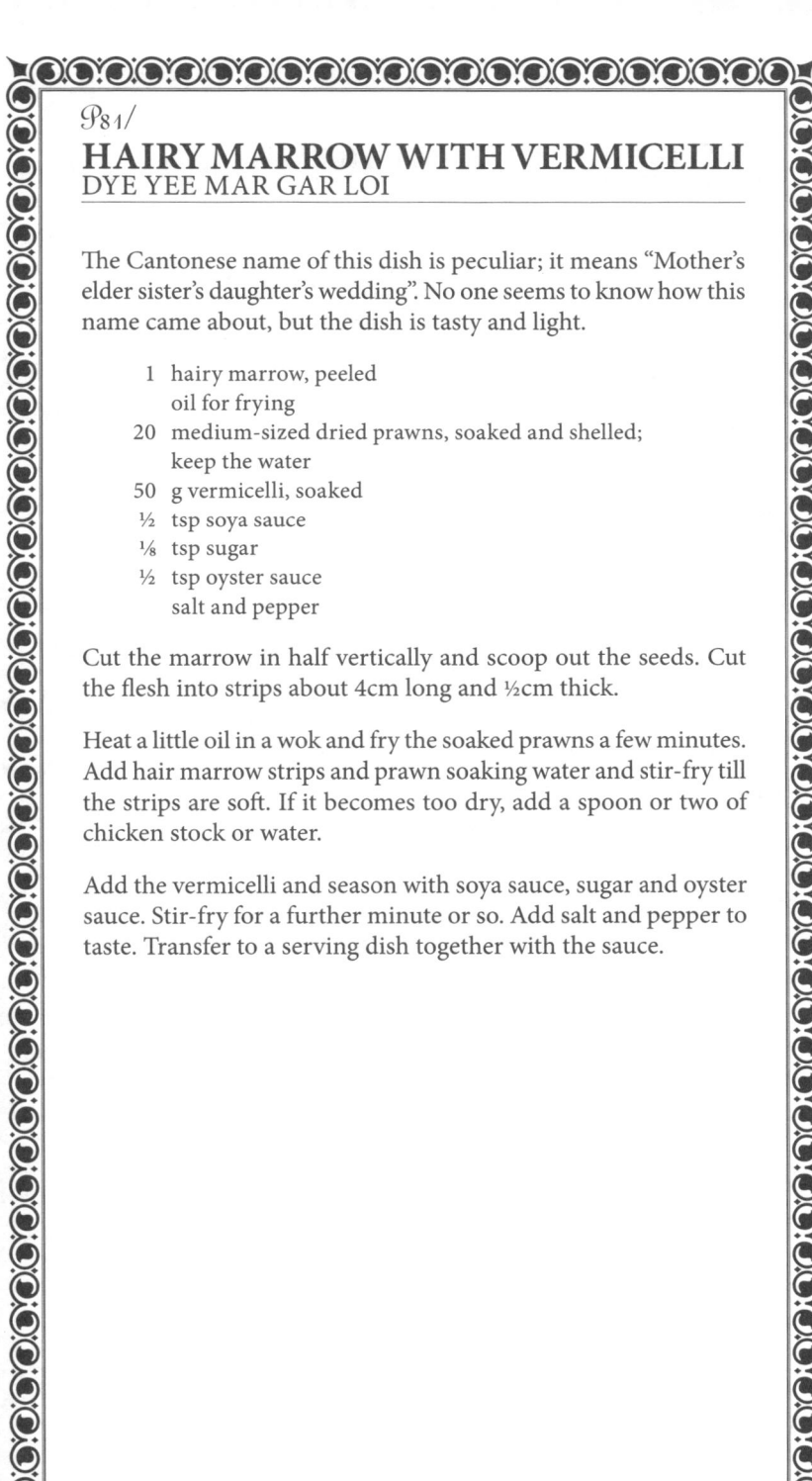

P81/
HAIRY MARROW WITH VERMICELLI
DYE YEE MAR GAR LOI

The Cantonese name of this dish is peculiar; it means "Mother's elder sister's daughter's wedding". No one seems to know how this name came about, but the dish is tasty and light.

- 1 hairy marrow, peeled
  oil for frying
- 20 medium-sized dried prawns, soaked and shelled; keep the water
- 50 g vermicelli, soaked
- ½ tsp soya sauce
- ⅛ tsp sugar
- ½ tsp oyster sauce
  salt and pepper

Cut the marrow in half vertically and scoop out the seeds. Cut the flesh into strips about 4cm long and ½cm thick.

Heat a little oil in a wok and fry the soaked prawns a few minutes. Add hair marrow strips and prawn soaking water and stir-fry till the strips are soft. If it becomes too dry, add a spoon or two of chicken stock or water.

Add the vermicelli and season with soya sauce, sugar and oyster sauce. Stir-fry for a further minute or so. Add salt and pepper to taste. Transfer to a serving dish together with the sauce.

STUFFED HAIRY MARROW
YONG JEET GUA

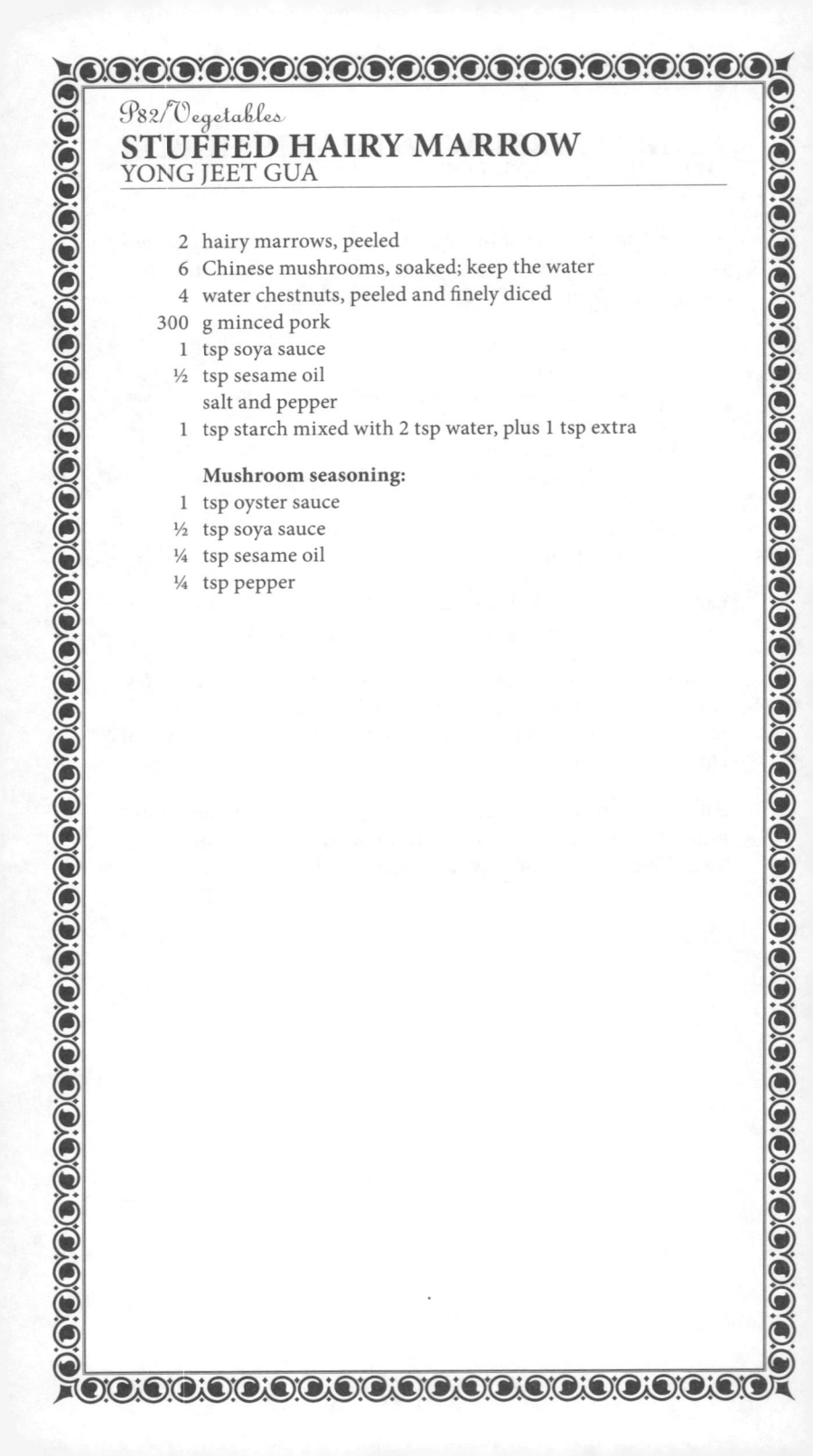

- 2 hairy marrows, peeled
- 6 Chinese mushrooms, soaked; keep the water
- 4 water chestnuts, peeled and finely diced
- 300 g minced pork
- 1 tsp soya sauce
- ½ tsp sesame oil
- salt and pepper
- 1 tsp starch mixed with 2 tsp water, plus 1 tsp extra

Mushroom seasoning:

- 1 tsp oyster sauce
- ½ tsp soya sauce
- ¼ tsp sesame oil
- ¼ tsp pepper

Cut off about 1cm from each end of the marrows and cut crosswise into 2cm thick sections. Cut away the pulp inside with a knife to form short tubes. Rub some starch on the inside and on the cut edges.

Simmer the mushrooms in a small saucepan with the soaking water and the mushroom seasoning until it is almost dry. Cool and dice finely.

Transfer the minced pork, diced mushrooms and water chestnuts to a bowl. Add the soya sauce, sesame oil, salt and pepper, and 1 teaspoon starch. Mix thoroughly.

Fill the tubes with the pork mixture and spread some stuffing over the cut edges.

Place in a deep dish, cut sides up and steam for 10-15 minutes.

Transfer the tubes to a serving plate and pour the juices into a small saucepan. To make a sauce, simmer and season with sesame oil, soya sauce, salt and pepper. Stir in the starch-mixture and continue to simmer until the sauce thickens a little, and pour it over the marrow.

Tip

If the stuffing is not enough to fill all the tubes, the unstuffed tubes can be thinly sliced and fried with a couple of beaten eggs.

Variation

Bitter gourds and cucumbers can be used for this dish, although they don't have the sweetness of hairy gourds. Zucchini, which were not available during Mother's time, would make an interesting change.

P84/Vegetables
BITTER GOURD OMELETTE
FOO GUA CHOW DARN

- 2-3 eggs, lightly beaten
- oil for frying
- 1 bitter gourd, halved, seeded and finely sliced
- 2 tbs crab meat, optional
- 2 tbs minced pork, optional
- 2 tbs stock
- salt and pepper

Season the eggs with salt and pepper to taste.

Heat some oil in a wok and stir-fry the gourd slices and stock for 2 minutes till almost dry.

Over high heat, add the eggs, crab and pork if using, and stir-fry until they are scrambled and the pork is cooked. The egg should be slightly wet. Transfer to a serving dish and serve immediately.

Variation

Other vegetables that can be fried with egg include carrots, hairy marrow, cucumber, and pumpkin. They need to be cut into strips of about 4cm long, 0.3cm wide. For carrots and hairy marrow, simmer the strips in a small saucepan with some stock until the strips are soft and the stock almost dry, before frying with egg.

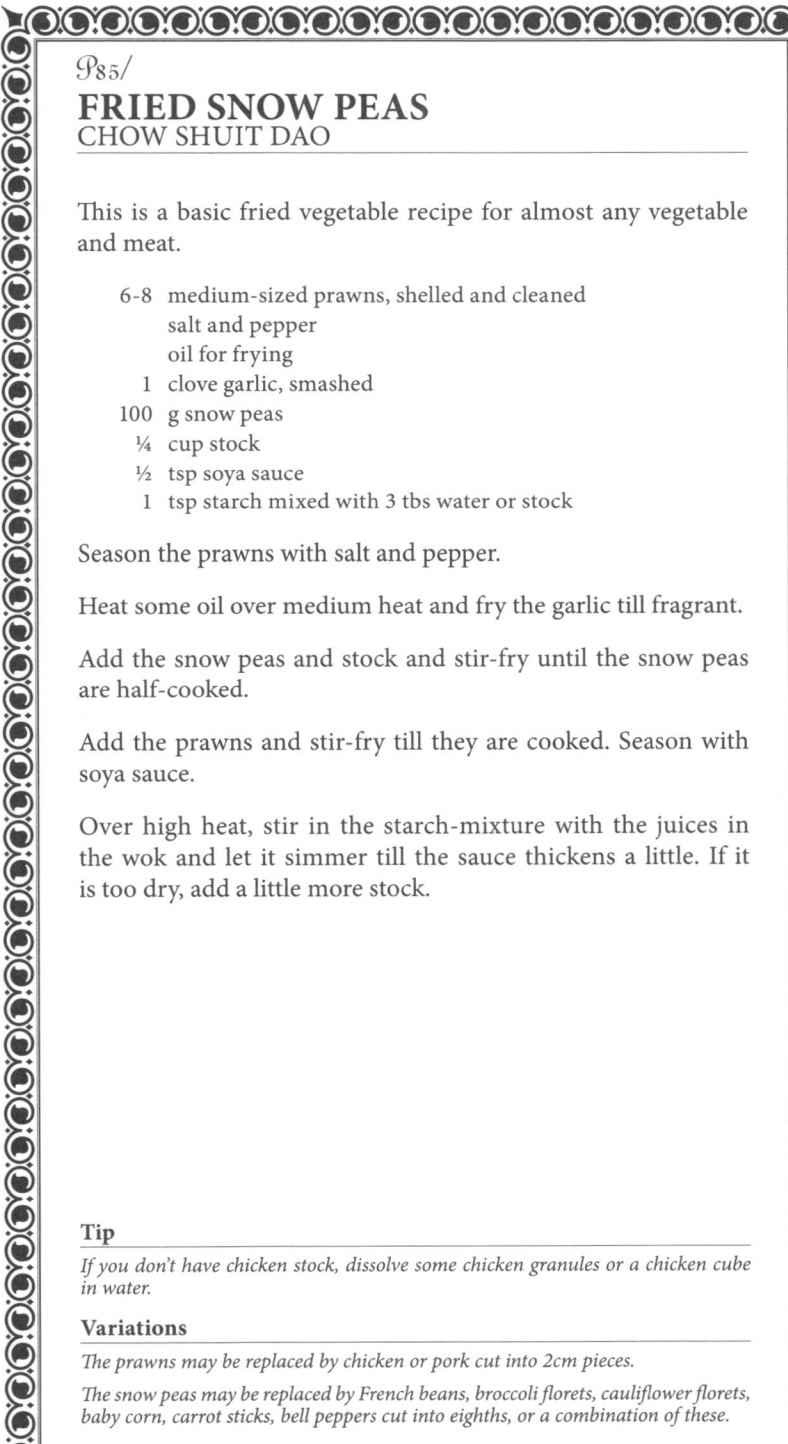

𝒫85/
FRIED SNOW PEAS
CHOW SHUIT DAO

This is a basic fried vegetable recipe for almost any vegetable and meat.

- 6-8 medium-sized prawns, shelled and cleaned
- salt and pepper
- oil for frying
- 1 clove garlic, smashed
- 100 g snow peas
- ¼ cup stock
- ½ tsp soya sauce
- 1 tsp starch mixed with 3 tbs water or stock

Season the prawns with salt and pepper.

Heat some oil over medium heat and fry the garlic till fragrant.

Add the snow peas and stock and stir-fry until the snow peas are half-cooked.

Add the prawns and stir-fry till they are cooked. Season with soya sauce.

Over high heat, stir in the starch-mixture with the juices in the wok and let it simmer till the sauce thickens a little. If it is too dry, add a little more stock.

Tip

If you don't have chicken stock, dissolve some chicken granules or a chicken cube in water.

Variations

The prawns may be replaced by chicken or pork cut into 2cm pieces.

The snow peas may be replaced by French beans, broccoli florets, cauliflower florets, baby corn, carrot sticks, bell peppers cut into eighths, or a combination of these.

POTATO CAKES
SHU JYE BANG

Vegetables

- 10 dried prawns, soaked and shelled
- 4 potatoes, peeled and thickly grated
- 1 egg
- ½ tsp starch
- salt and pepper
- oil for frying

Pound the prawns into a mash.

Mix the grated potatoes and mashed prawns. Add the egg and starch and season with salt and pepper. Stir to mix.

Heat some oil in a wok over medium heat. Scoop 1 heaped teaspoon of the potato mixture into the wok and flatten it into a patty. If it spreads too much, add a little more starch to the mix. Turn it over after a couple of minutes and continue frying till it is golden brown. Taste the fried cake and season the remaining mixture accordingly.

Continue frying the rest of the mixture, no more than 2 or 3 cakes at a time. Serve with chilli sauce.

Variation

Instead of potatoes, you may use yam, sweet potatoes or Chinese potatoes.

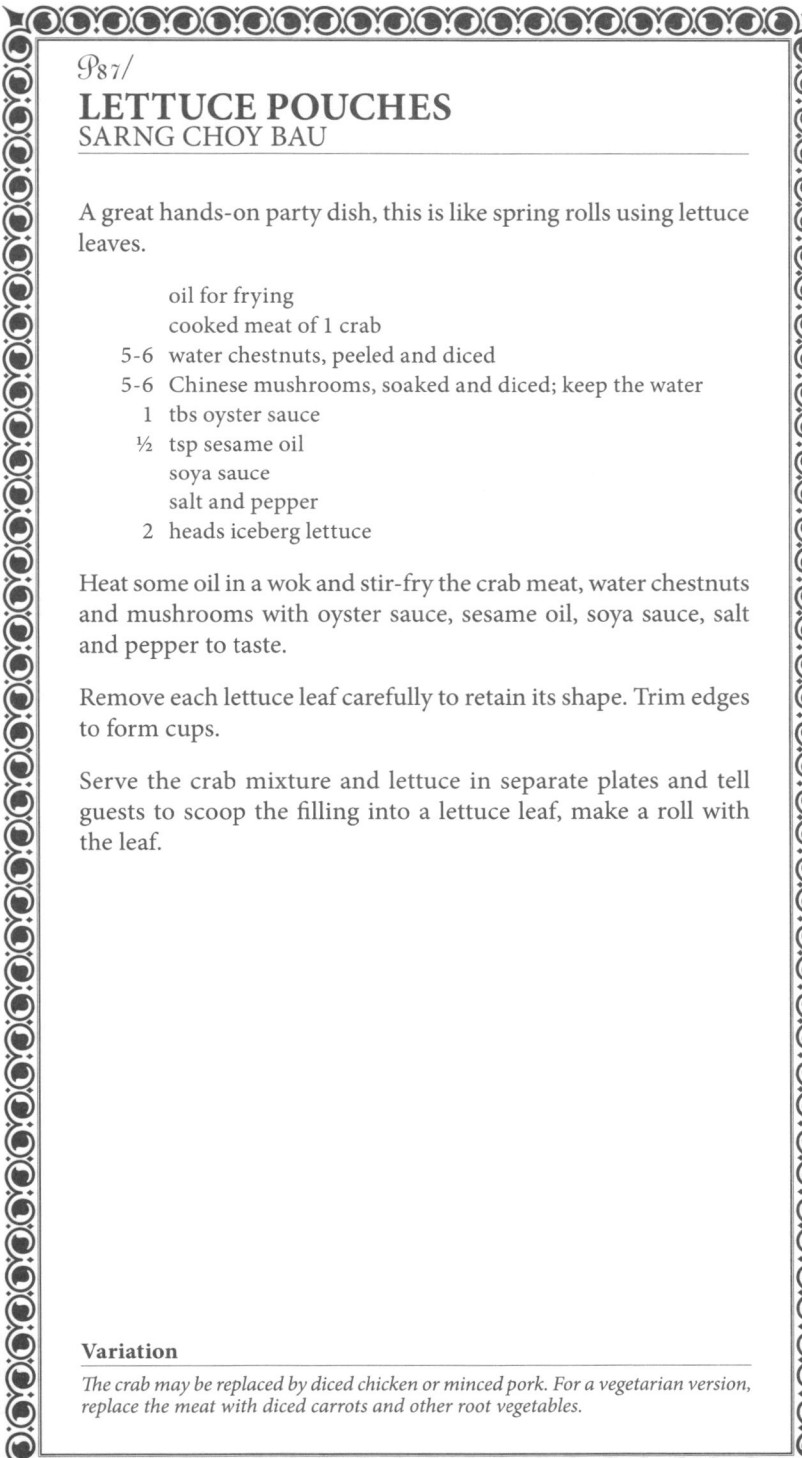

℘87/
LETTUCE POUCHES
SARNG CHOY BAU

A great hands-on party dish, this is like spring rolls using lettuce leaves.

	oil for frying
	cooked meat of 1 crab
5-6	water chestnuts, peeled and diced
5-6	Chinese mushrooms, soaked and diced; keep the water
1	tbs oyster sauce
½	tsp sesame oil
	soya sauce
	salt and pepper
2	heads iceberg lettuce

Heat some oil in a wok and stir-fry the crab meat, water chestnuts and mushrooms with oyster sauce, sesame oil, soya sauce, salt and pepper to taste.

Remove each lettuce leaf carefully to retain its shape. Trim edges to form cups.

Serve the crab mixture and lettuce in separate plates and tell guests to scoop the filling into a lettuce leaf, make a roll with the leaf.

Variation

The crab may be replaced by diced chicken or minced pork. For a vegetarian version, replace the meat with diced carrots and other root vegetables.

CHINESE NEW YEAR RAW FISH
LOU HEI

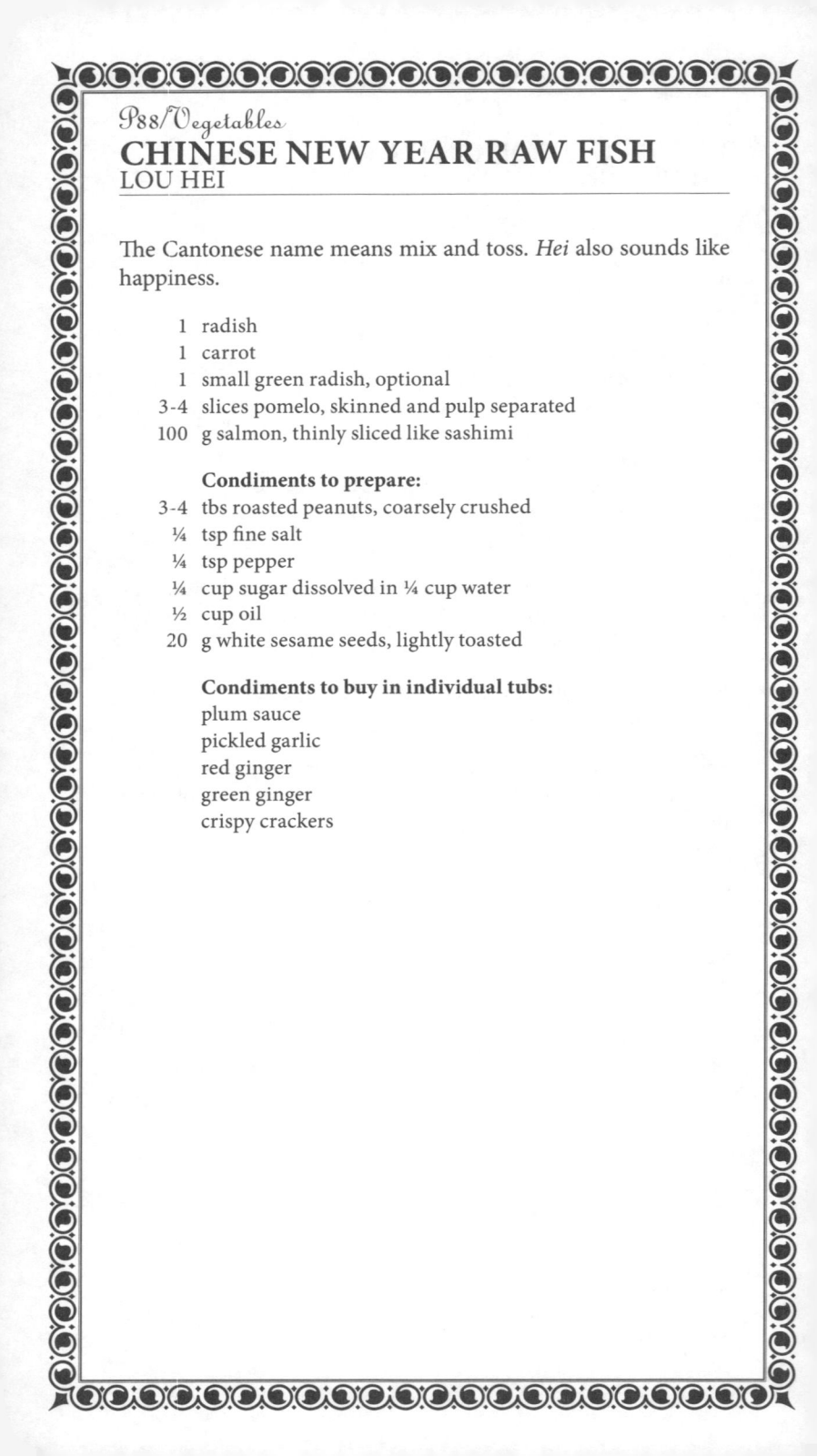

P88/Vegetables

The Cantonese name means mix and toss. *Hei* also sounds like happiness.

- 1 radish
- 1 carrot
- 1 small green radish, optional
- 3-4 slices pomelo, skinned and pulp separated
- 100 g salmon, thinly sliced like sashimi

Condiments to prepare:
- 3-4 tbs roasted peanuts, coarsely crushed
- ¼ tsp fine salt
- ¼ tsp pepper
- ¼ cup sugar dissolved in ¼ cup water
- ½ cup oil
- 20 g white sesame seeds, lightly toasted

Condiments to buy in individual tubs:
plum sauce
pickled garlic
red ginger
green ginger
crispy crackers

Cut the vegetables into long thin strips. Wrap large handfuls in clean cloth and wring dry.

Arrange a big pile of radish in the middle of a large plate with smaller piles of carrots and green radish on either side. Around this, place the red and green ginger and pomelo pulp in small piles.

Put the crushed peanuts, the salt and pepper, sugar syrup and oil in separate small dishes. The rest of the bought condiments may remain in their individual containers, uncovered, or transfered into dishes.

Serve the large plate of vegetables surrounded by the small dishes of condiments.

Arrange the salmon slices on a plate.

The ritual

As each condiment is poured onto the vegetables, say a Chinese phrase for good luck:

Salmon: leen leen yao yu – May there be abundance ever year
Cooking oil: shuen shuen lei lei – May everything go smoothly
Syrup and plum sauce: teem teem mutt mutt – May all be sweet and loving
Crispy bits: moon dei gum cheen – May gold and money cover the whole floor
Salt and pepper: marn see yu yee – May all things come easily
Sesame seeds: sarng yee heng loong – May business flourish
Peanuts: chuet yup peng on – May there be peace in and out of this home
Pickled garlic: sun tai geen hong – May we enjoy good health

With that, everyone pitches in to toss the vegetables with chopsticks, shouting "lo hei, lo hei," and any of the above sayings.

Actually, only the first four sayings correspond to the respective condiments. The rest can be said with whichever of the other four condiments being added. These sayings are also used to greet people during the Chinese New Year season.

And it does not really matter which order the condiments are added.

FRIED EGG PACKETS
JEEN DARN GOK

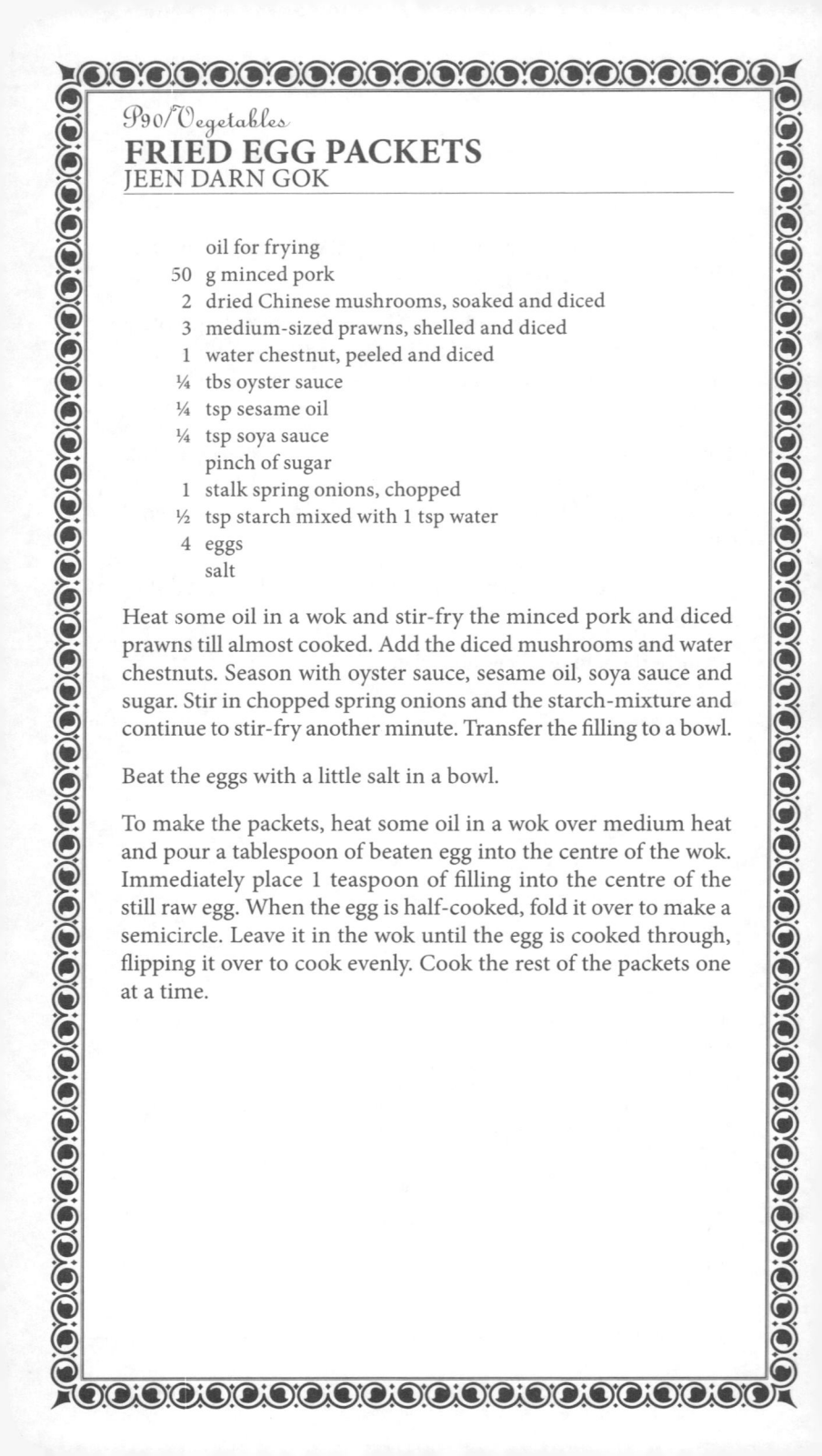

- oil for frying
- 50 g minced pork
- 2 dried Chinese mushrooms, soaked and diced
- 3 medium-sized prawns, shelled and diced
- 1 water chestnut, peeled and diced
- ¼ tbs oyster sauce
- ¼ tsp sesame oil
- ¼ tsp soya sauce
- pinch of sugar
- 1 stalk spring onions, chopped
- ½ tsp starch mixed with 1 tsp water
- 4 eggs
- salt

Heat some oil in a wok and stir-fry the minced pork and diced prawns till almost cooked. Add the diced mushrooms and water chestnuts. Season with oyster sauce, sesame oil, soya sauce and sugar. Stir in chopped spring onions and the starch-mixture and continue to stir-fry another minute. Transfer the filling to a bowl.

Beat the eggs with a little salt in a bowl.

To make the packets, heat some oil in a wok over medium heat and pour a tablespoon of beaten egg into the centre of the wok. Immediately place 1 teaspoon of filling into the centre of the still raw egg. When the egg is half-cooked, fold it over to make a semicircle. Leave it in the wok until the egg is cooked through, flipping it over to cook evenly. Cook the rest of the packets one at a time.

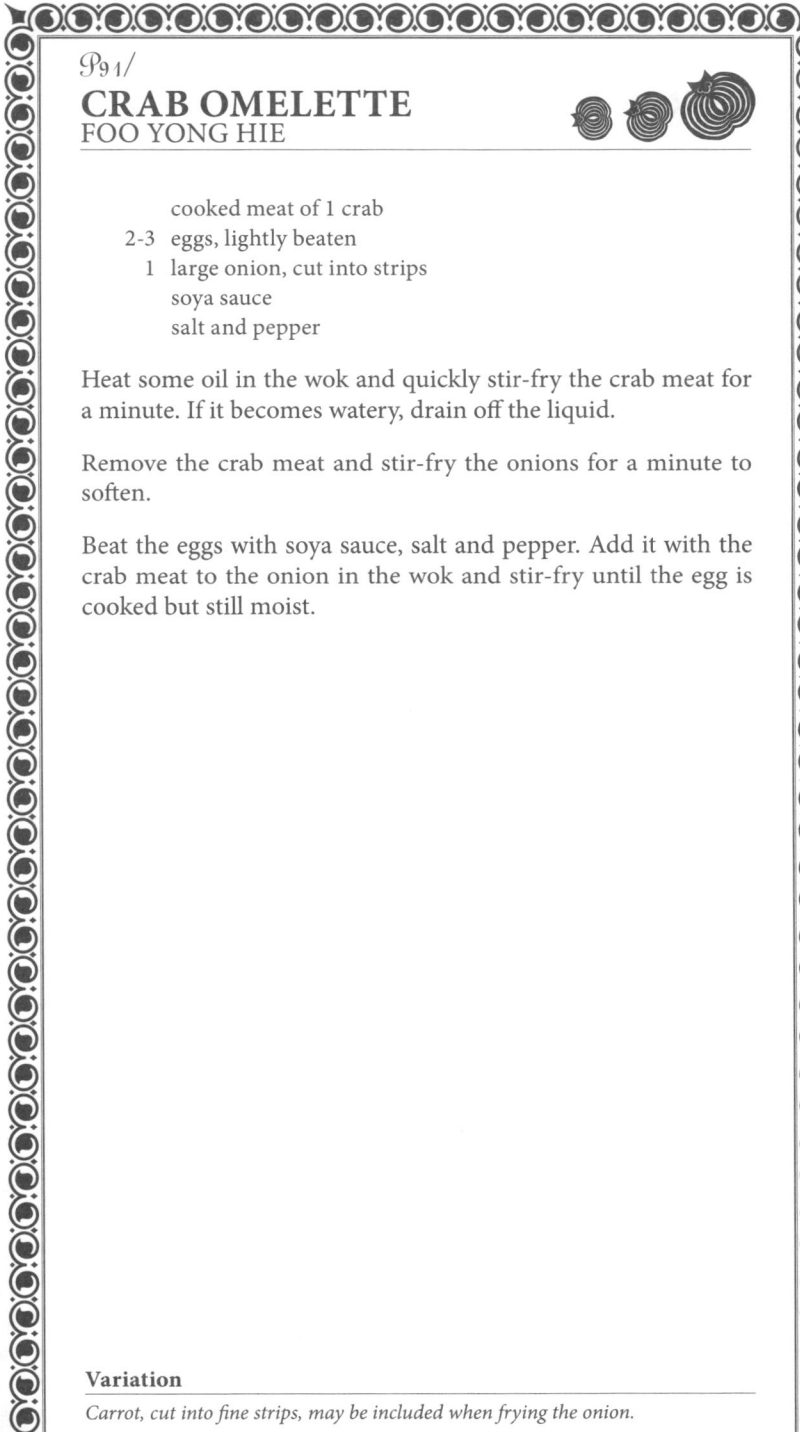

91/
CRAB OMELETTE
FOO YONG HIE

	cooked meat of 1 crab
2-3	eggs, lightly beaten
1	large onion, cut into strips
	soya sauce
	salt and pepper

Heat some oil in the wok and quickly stir-fry the crab meat for a minute. If it becomes watery, drain off the liquid.

Remove the crab meat and stir-fry the onions for a minute to soften.

Beat the eggs with soya sauce, salt and pepper. Add it with the crab meat to the onion in the wok and stir-fry until the egg is cooked but still moist.

Variation

Carrot, cut into fine strips, may be included when frying the onion.

THREE-EGG STEAMED CUSTARD
SARM WONG DARN

- 2 eggs
- 2 salted eggs
- oil for rubbing and drizzling
- 2 century eggs

Beat the eggs and the whites of the salted eggs together in a bowl. Note the level of the egg on the side of the bowl. Pour the egg mixture into a large bowl and add water equal to one and three-quarters the amount of the egg mixture. Combine with the egg mixture and beat to mix thoroughly.

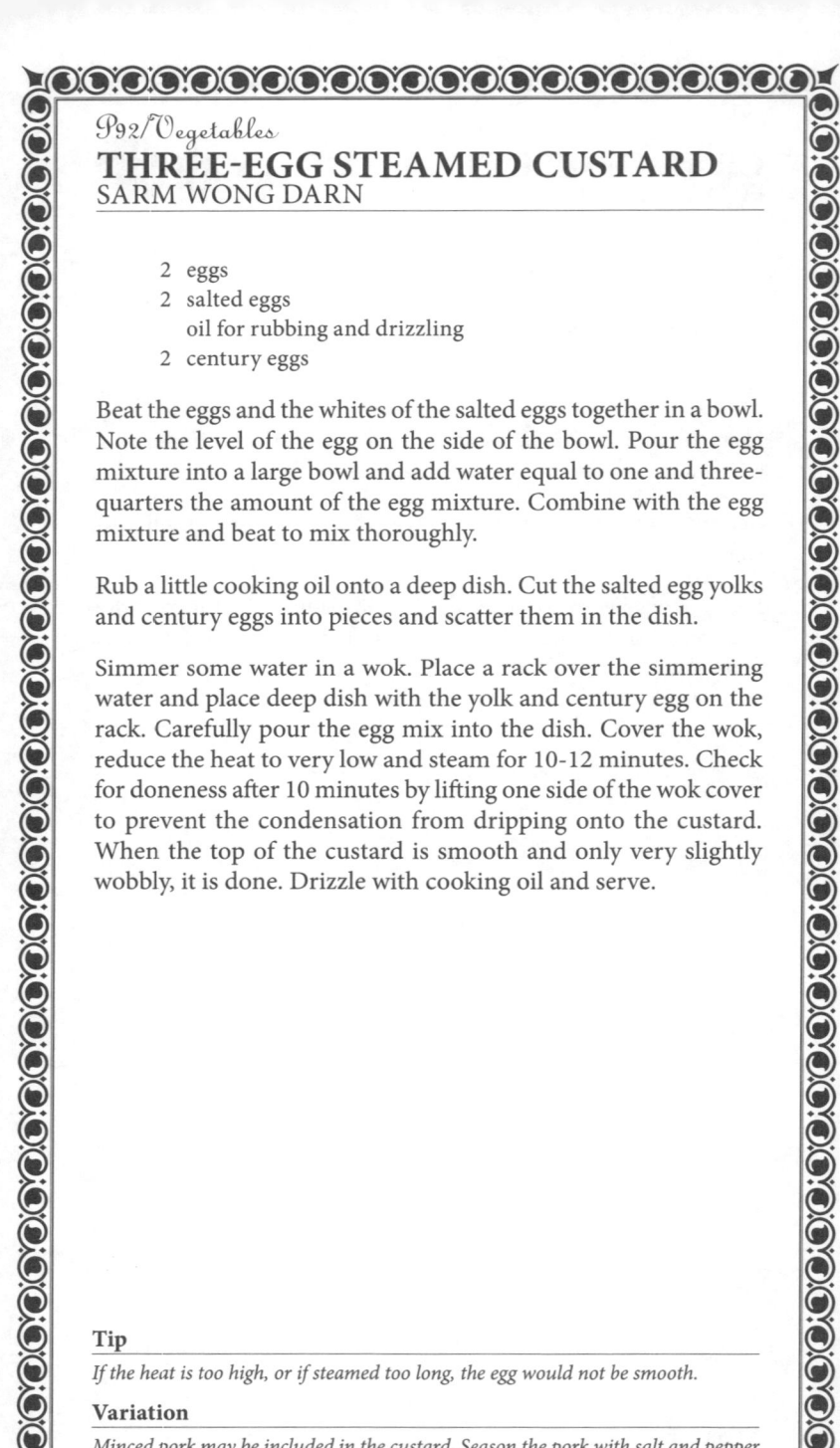

Rub a little cooking oil onto a deep dish. Cut the salted egg yolks and century eggs into pieces and scatter them in the dish.

Simmer some water in a wok. Place a rack over the simmering water and place deep dish with the yolk and century egg on the rack. Carefully pour the egg mix into the dish. Cover the wok, reduce the heat to very low and steam for 10-12 minutes. Check for doneness after 10 minutes by lifting one side of the wok cover to prevent the condensation from dripping onto the custard. When the top of the custard is smooth and only very slightly wobbly, it is done. Drizzle with cooking oil and serve.

Tip

If the heat is too high, or if steamed too long, the egg would not be smooth.

Variation

Minced pork may be included in the custard. Season the pork with salt and pepper and scatter small amounts among the egg pieces.

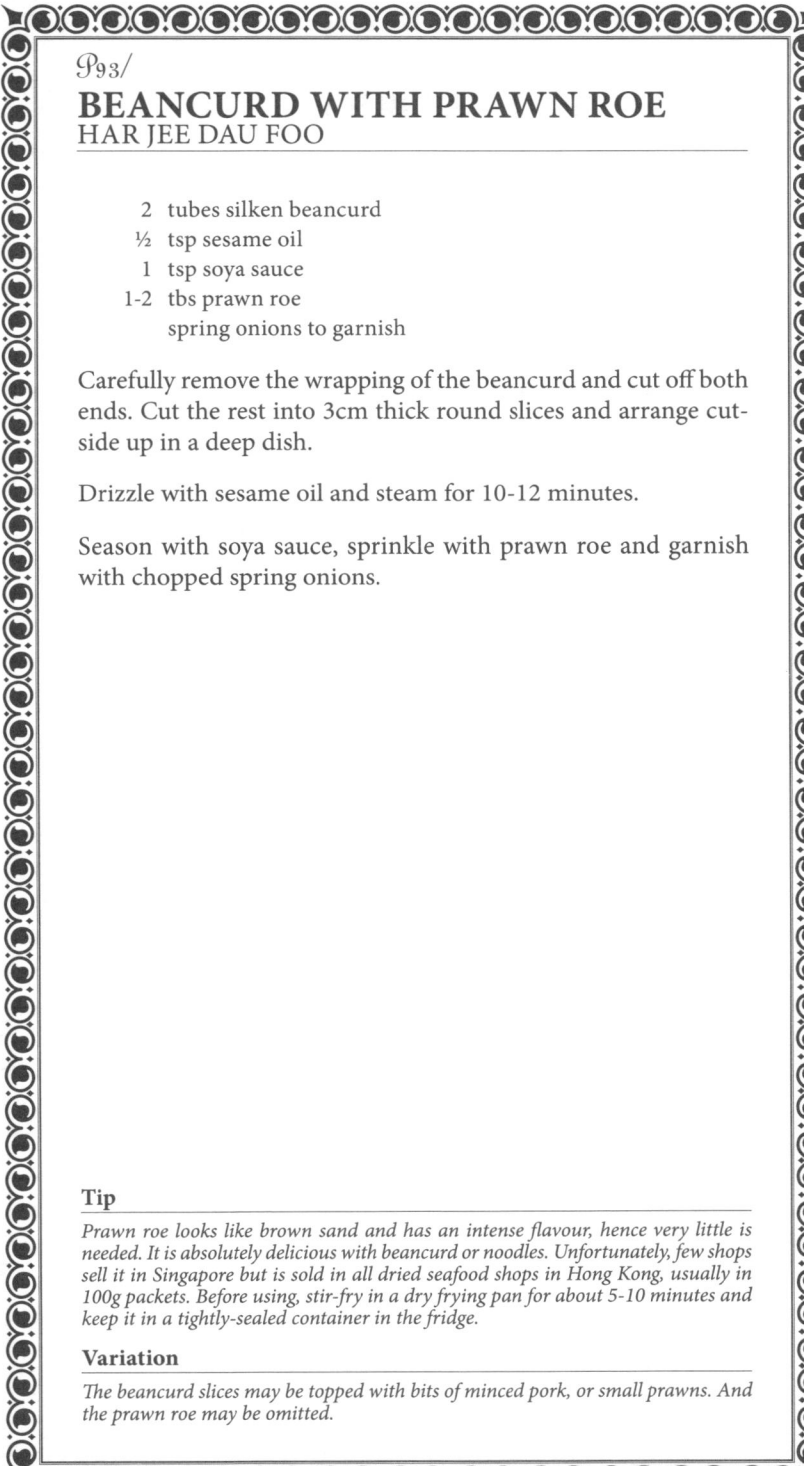

P93/
BEANCURD WITH PRAWN ROE
HAR JEE DAU FOO

- 2 tubes silken beancurd
- ½ tsp sesame oil
- 1 tsp soya sauce
- 1-2 tbs prawn roe
- spring onions to garnish

Carefully remove the wrapping of the beancurd and cut off both ends. Cut the rest into 3cm thick round slices and arrange cut-side up in a deep dish.

Drizzle with sesame oil and steam for 10-12 minutes.

Season with soya sauce, sprinkle with prawn roe and garnish with chopped spring onions.

Tip

Prawn roe looks like brown sand and has an intense flavour, hence very little is needed. It is absolutely delicious with beancurd or noodles. Unfortunately, few shops sell it in Singapore but is sold in all dried seafood shops in Hong Kong, usually in 100g packets. Before using, stir-fry in a dry frying pan for about 5-10 minutes and keep it in a tightly-sealed container in the fridge.

Variation

The beancurd slices may be topped with bits of minced pork, or small prawns. And the prawn roe may be omitted.

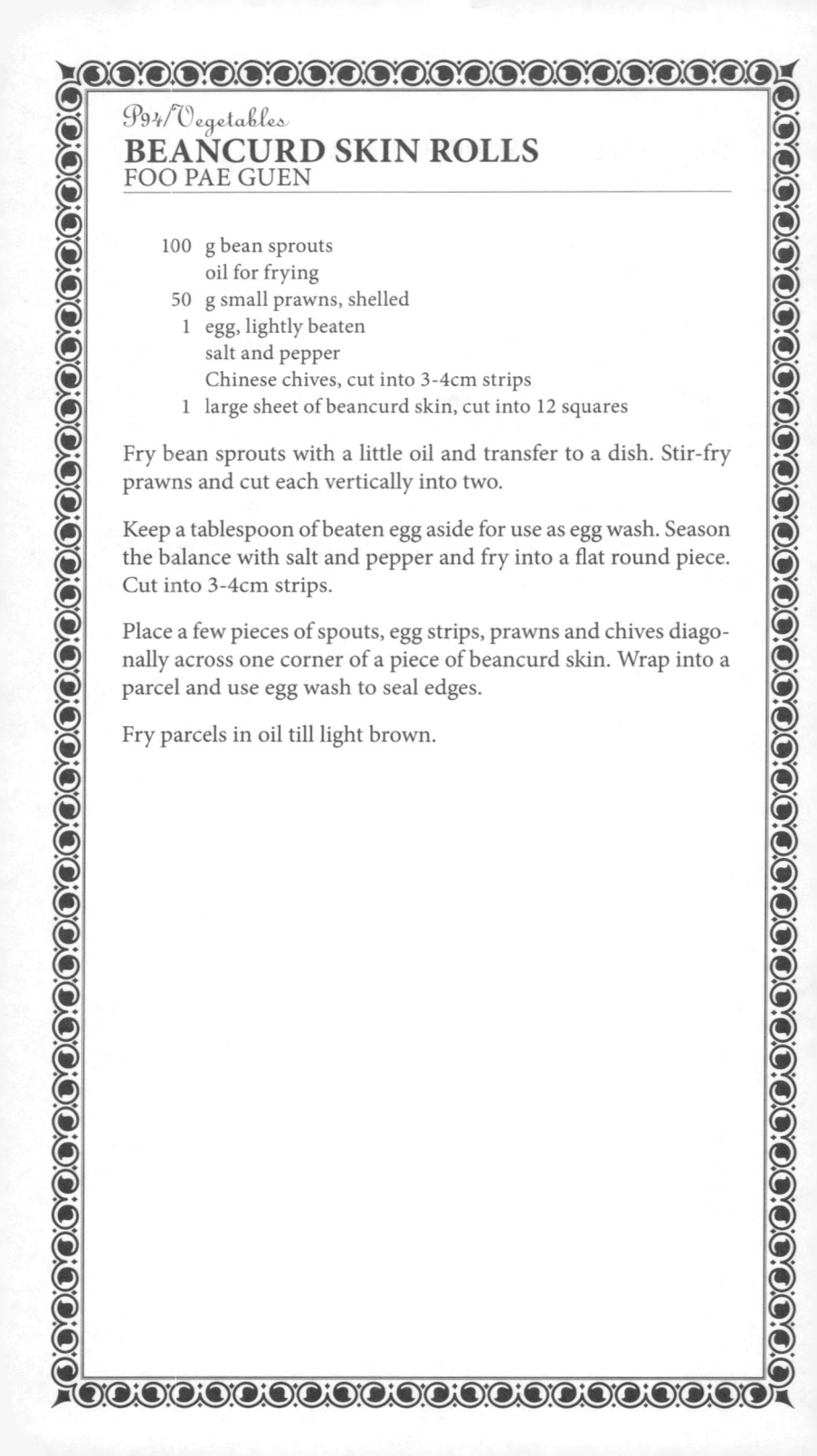

BEANCURD SKIN ROLLS
FOO PAE GUEN

- 100 g bean sprouts
- oil for frying
- 50 g small prawns, shelled
- 1 egg, lightly beaten
- salt and pepper
- Chinese chives, cut into 3-4cm strips
- 1 large sheet of beancurd skin, cut into 12 squares

Fry bean sprouts with a little oil and transfer to a dish. Stir-fry prawns and cut each vertically into two.

Keep a tablespoon of beaten egg aside for use as egg wash. Season the balance with salt and pepper and fry into a flat round piece. Cut into 3-4cm strips.

Place a few pieces of spouts, egg strips, prawns and chives diagonally across one corner of a piece of beancurd skin. Wrap into a parcel and use egg wash to seal edges.

Fry parcels in oil till light brown.

℘95/
STUFFED DRIED BEANCURD
YONG TEEM JOKE

- 10 pieces dried beancurd, soaked
  starch for dusting
- 100 g fish paste
  oil for frying

Cut the beancurd pieces in half to make 20 squares.

Dust one side of the beancurd squares with starch. Spread ½cm thick with fish paste onto the starched side of one piece and cover with another piece, starched side down and press the two together to flatten the sandwich evenly. Fill the rest of the pieces similarly.

Heat 4-5 tablespoons oil in a frying pan enough to half-cover the stuffed beancurd. Fry over medium heat until brown and crisp. Turn over to fry other side.

Tips

Dried beancurd comes in packets of 5 or 6 brown sheets, each about 12cm by 4cm and 2mm thick. If buying loose pieces from dried good store, choose those that are smooth and less thick.

Fish paste is sold in wet markets at the stalls that sell fish balls and fish cake.

EIGHT TREASURES BEANCURD
BART BO DAU FOO

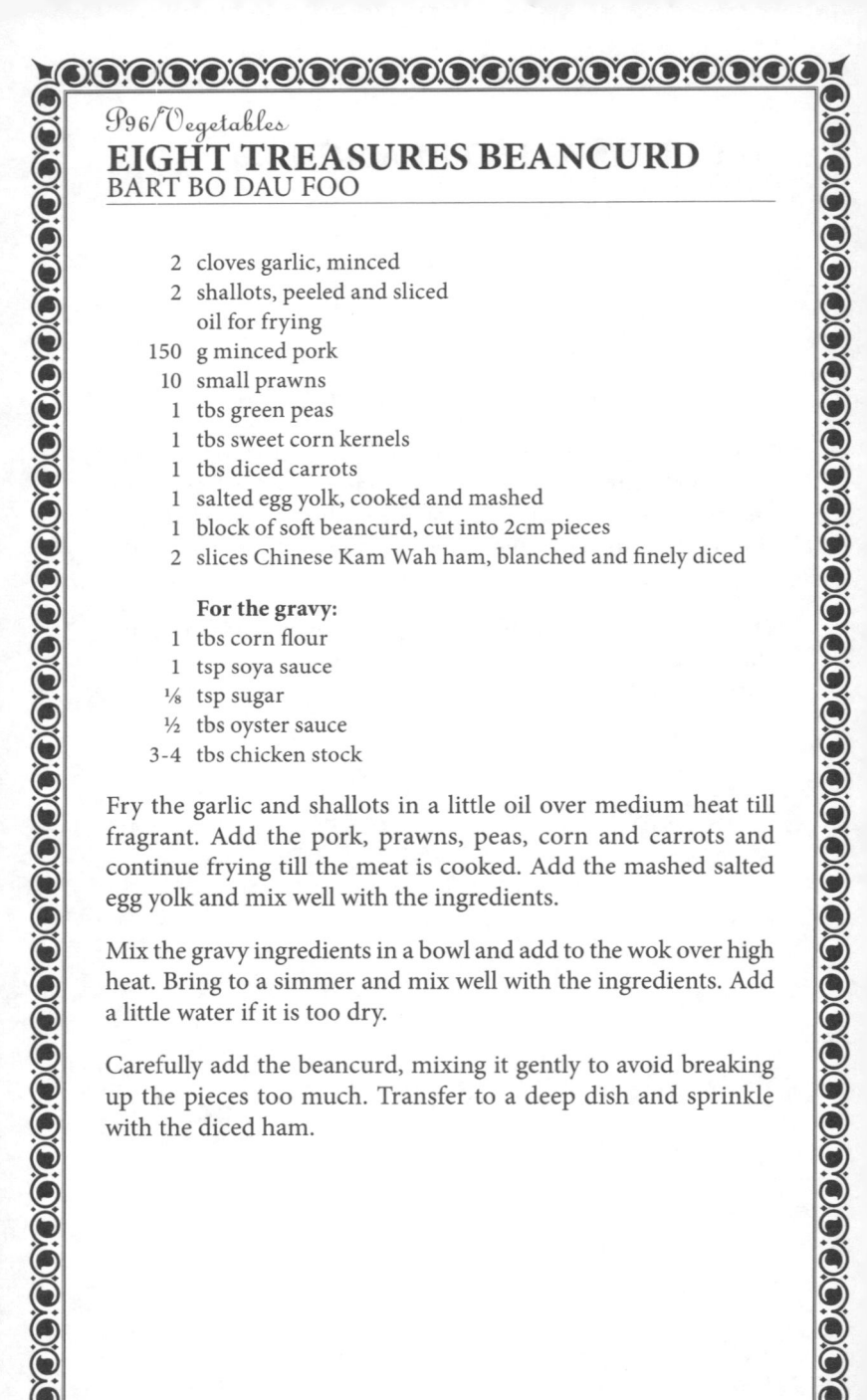

- 2 cloves garlic, minced
- 2 shallots, peeled and sliced
- oil for frying
- 150 g minced pork
- 10 small prawns
- 1 tbs green peas
- 1 tbs sweet corn kernels
- 1 tbs diced carrots
- 1 salted egg yolk, cooked and mashed
- 1 block of soft beancurd, cut into 2cm pieces
- 2 slices Chinese Kam Wah ham, blanched and finely diced

For the gravy:
- 1 tbs corn flour
- 1 tsp soya sauce
- 1/8 tsp sugar
- 1/2 tbs oyster sauce
- 3-4 tbs chicken stock

Fry the garlic and shallots in a little oil over medium heat till fragrant. Add the pork, prawns, peas, corn and carrots and continue frying till the meat is cooked. Add the mashed salted egg yolk and mix well with the ingredients.

Mix the gravy ingredients in a bowl and add to the wok over high heat. Bring to a simmer and mix well with the ingredients. Add a little water if it is too dry.

Carefully add the beancurd, mixing it gently to avoid breaking up the pieces too much. Transfer to a deep dish and sprinkle with the diced ham.

P97/
STUFFED BITTER GOURD
YONG FOO GUA

- 1 bitter gourd
- starch for rubbing
- 300 g mackerel meat
- oil for frying

Sauce:
- 2 tbs stock
- 1 tsp soya sauce
- 1 tsp dark sauce
- 1 tbs oyster sauce
- 1/8 tsp sugar
- 1 tsp corn flour

Cut the bitter gourd into 1cm thick slices. Discard the two pointed ends. Remove the seeds and rub the inside of each ring with starch.

Press 1-2 tablespoons of fish meat into the ring to fill the hole. Smoothen the meat over the edge of the ring. Repeat with the rest of the rings.

Heat some oil in a wok over medium heat and fry 4 to 5 slices at a time until light brown and the fish is cooked through. Alternatively, the slices may be steamed for about 10 minutes.

To make the sauce, simmer the sauce ingredients in a saucepan while stirring until it is thickened and smooth. If it is too thick, add a little stock. If it is too thin, simmer longer to reduce to the right consistency.

Transfer the slices into a serving dish and pour the sauce over.

Tip

Mackerel meat is sold in the wet markets, usually at the stalls that sell beancurd and uncooked noodles. The meat is already mixed into fish cakes which are still raw but seasoned.

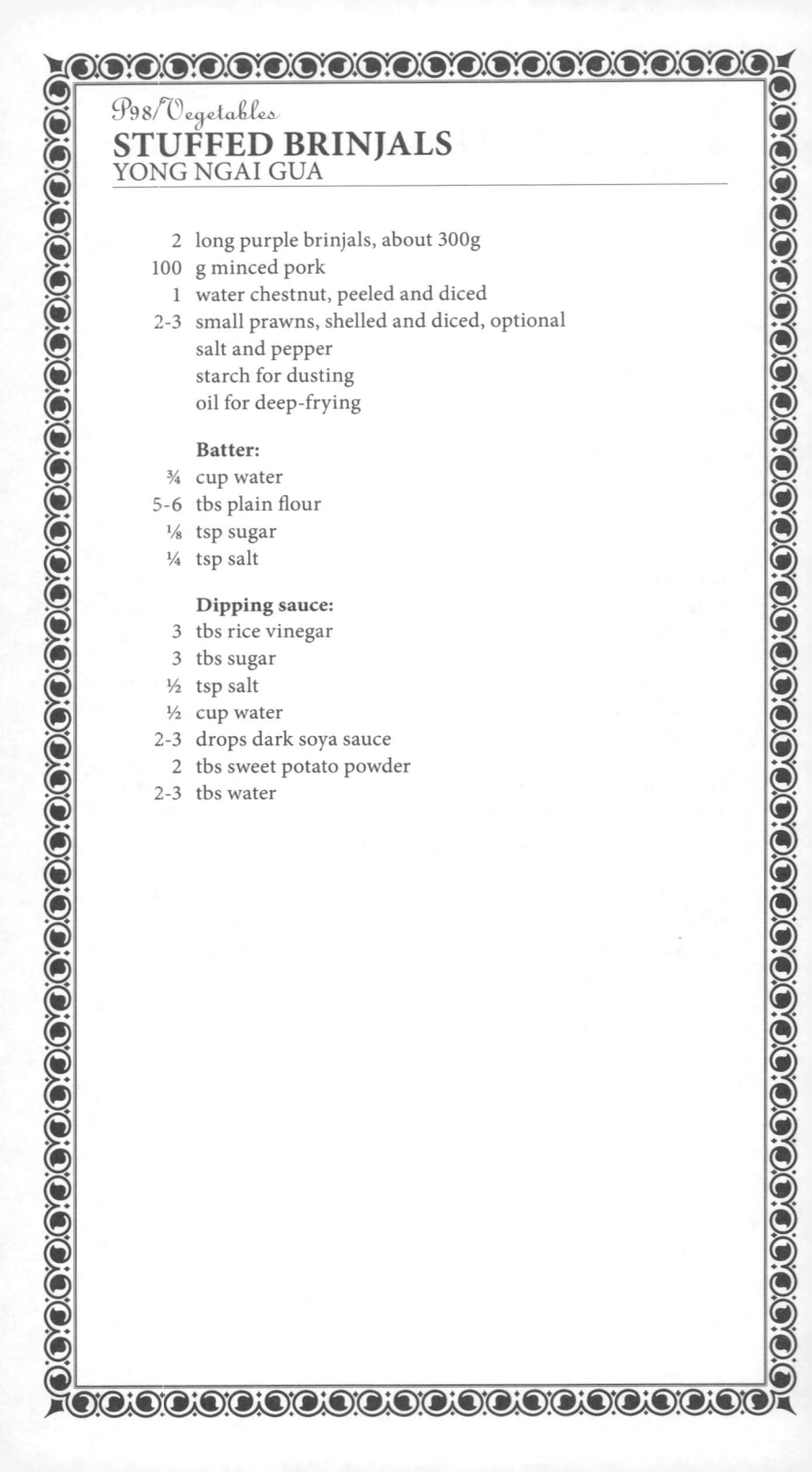

STUFFED BRINJALS
YONG NGAI GUA

- 2 long purple brinjals, about 300g
- 100 g minced pork
- 1 water chestnut, peeled and diced
- 2-3 small prawns, shelled and diced, optional
- salt and pepper
- starch for dusting
- oil for deep-frying

Batter:
- ¾ cup water
- 5-6 tbs plain flour
- ⅛ tsp sugar
- ¼ tsp salt

Dipping sauce:
- 3 tbs rice vinegar
- 3 tbs sugar
- ½ tsp salt
- ½ cup water
- 2-3 drops dark soya sauce
- 2 tbs sweet potato powder
- 2-3 tbs water

Cut the brinjals into 1cm thick slices. Discard both ends. Make a slit about ¾ ways into each slice.

Mix the pork, water chestnut and prawn if using and season with salt and pepper. Stir until the mixture is sticky.

Smear some starch inside the slits. Press about a teaspoon of meat mixture into each slit and smoothen the edge. Dust the edge with starch.

To make the batter, mix all the ingredients and stir into a smooth paste. It should have the consistency of pouring cream.

Dip a piece of stuffed brinjal in the batter and deep-fry till golden brown. Fry only 4 or 5 pieces at a time to avoid over crowding the pan.

To make the sauce, pour the vinegar, sugar, salt and water into a bowl and stir to dissolve the sugar. Add the dark soya sauce to give it a deep golden colour.

Transfer to a small saucepan and bring the liquid to a simmer. Add the sweet potato powder a little at a time, stirring after each addition. Stop adding when it thickens a little. It will become thicker when cool. If it is too thick, add a little water.

Serve the stuffed brinjals immediately after frying with the sauce in a separate bowl.

Tip

Large round brinjals may be used, but the slices will be very big and a lot more pork will be needed.

Actual size

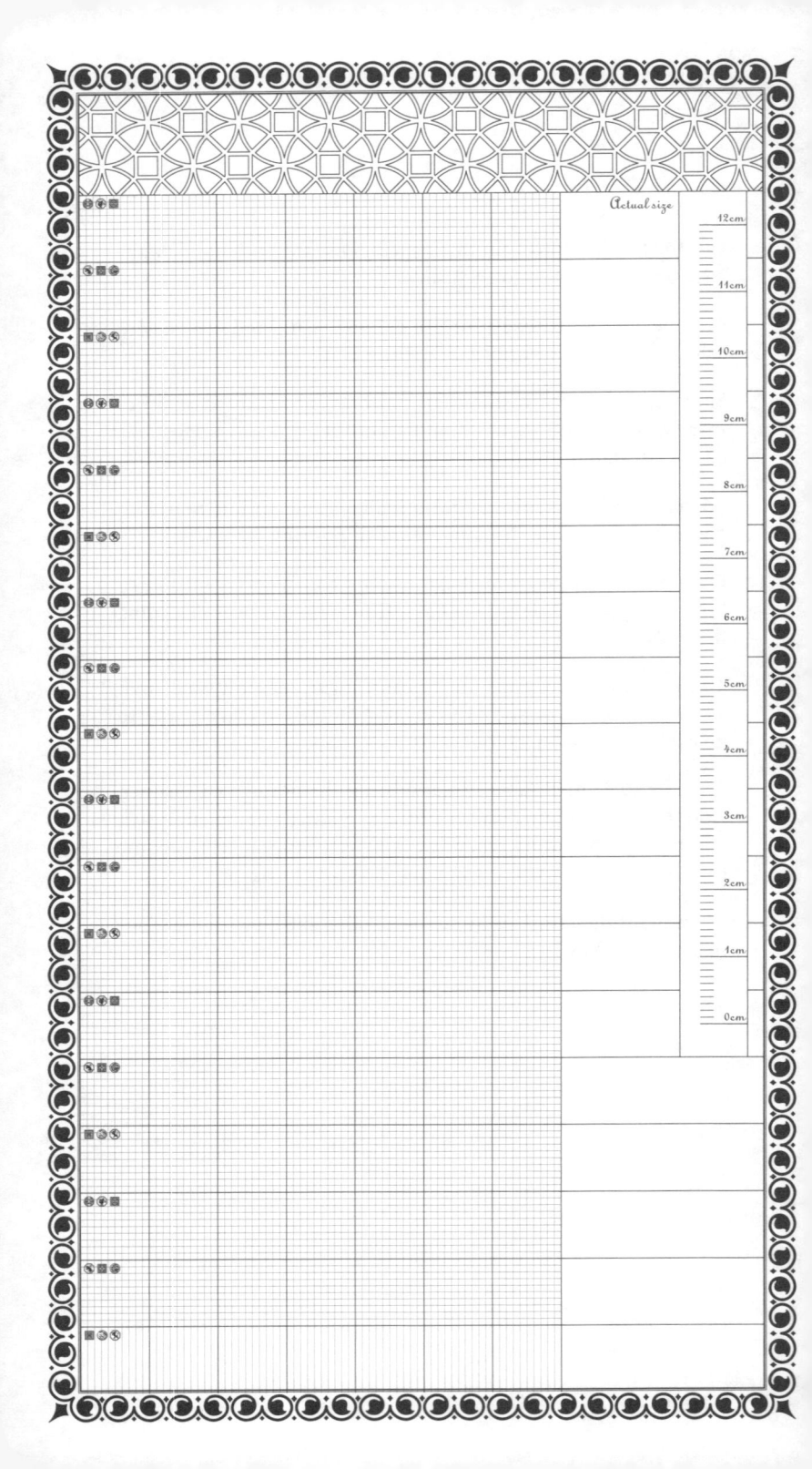

12cm
11cm
10cm
9cm
8cm
7cm
6cm
5cm
4cm
3cm
2cm
1cm
0cm

Rice & Noodles

P102/Rice & Noodles
FRIED RICE
CHOW FARN

	oil for frying
1	large onion, chopped
2-3	cloves garlic, minced
3	tbs green peas
3-4	tbs sweet corn, optional
1	small carrot, peeled and diced, optional
2	Chinese sausages, diced
6	medium-sized prawns, shelled and diced
	cooked meat of ½ crab, optional
2-3	cups cold cooked rice
2	tbs stock
1	tbs dark soya sauce
	soya sauce
	salt and pepper
2	eggs, lightly beaten, seasoned
	spring onions, celery leaves and strips of chilli to garnish

Heat in a little oil in a wok over medium heat and fry onions and garlic till fragrant. Toss in the vegetables and fry till they are slightly soft. Add the sausages and fry till the pieces begin to brown. Add the prawns and fry till they are done. Finally, add the crab meat and fry for a few seconds.

Add the rice and 2 tablespoons of stock and fry to break up the clumps of rice and mix with the ingredients, adding soya sauce, dark sauce, salt and pepper to taste.

Move the rice to the side and add a tablespoon of oil to the bottom of the wok. Turn up the heat and pour the beaten egg into the oil. Stir the rice over the egg and fry to mix well.

Transfer to a serving plate, top with garnish and serve immediately.

Tip

Almost any meat or vegetables diced can be added to this. Other ingredients that could go into the fried rice are barbeque pork (char siew), chicken, diced French or long beans.

$P_{103}/$
GLUTINOUS RICE
LOR MYE FARN

- 5 Chinese mushrooms, soaked; keep the water
- 500 g uncooked glutinous rice, soaked overnight
- 4 shallots
- 1 Chinese sausage, diced
- 10-12 dried prawns, soaked and finely diced
- 2 tbs oil
- 6-8 cups water
- ½ tsp dark soya sauce
- soya sauce
- pepper

Mushroom seasoning:
- ¼ tsp salt
- ¼ tsp soya sauce
- ¼ tsp sesame oil
- ¼ tsp sugar
- ½ tsp oyster sauce

Place the mushrooms and its soaking water into a small saucepan with the mushroom seasoning. Simmer till the sauce is almost dry. Dice the mushrooms.

Mix the soaked rice with the mushrooms shallots, Chinese sausage and dried prawns in a wok with the oil and stir-fry over medium heat. Add a tablespoon of water and the dark soya sauce and continue frying. Carry on adding water and frying until the rice is half-cooked and the grains are still hard in the centre.

Transfer into a large bowl and steam 20-25 minutes. Stir the rice thoroughly, scraping from the bottom and separating the grains. Season with soya sauce and pepper to taste. Continue steaming and adding water until the rice is cooked through.

P104/Rice & Noodles
ONE-POT CHICKEN RICE
GYE FARN

This is one of the easiest recipes. The seasoning of the mushrooms may seem bothersome but Mother says that Chinese mushrooms need to be "fed", to give them some taste before adding to a dish.

- 2 chicken thighs with drumsticks, boned and cut into 2cm pieces
- ½ tbs oyster sauce
- ¼ tsp sesame oil
- ¼ tsp soya sauce
- ½ tsp dark soya sauce
- ¼ tsp sugar
- dash of pepper
- ½ cm piece of ginger, grated
- ½ tsp brandy or Chinese cooking wine
- 3-4 dried Chinese mushrooms, soaked and diced
- 1 Chinese sausage, diced
- 1½ cups uncooked rice

Mushroom seasoning:
- ¼ tsp oyster sauce
- soya sauce
- pepper

Marinate the chicken with the oyster sauce, sesame oil, soya sauce, pepper and ginger and brandy and set aside.

Place diced mushrooms and soaking water in a small saucepan with the oyster sauce, soya sauce and pepper. Simmer until the sauce is almost dry.

Mix the mushrooms with the marinated chicken.

Cook the rice in a rice cooker. Half way during the cooking, when the grains are still wet, pour the chicken and mushrooms with all the seasoning into the rice and give it a quick but thorough stir. Replace the lid and let the cooking continue till the rice is done.

Variation

You may include diced cooked pork or duck. A few small pieces of salted fish will also enhance the taste. When the rice is cooked, you may lay some green vegetable on top and cover for another 5 minutes.

P105/
CHICKEN CONGEE
GYE JOKE

Cooking this in a slow cooker takes patience. Cook it overnight if you want it for breakfast.

- 200 g lean pork, blanched and sliced
- salt
- 200 g chicken meat in 1-2 cm pieces
- soya sauce
- 1½ cups uncooked rice
- 7 cups chicken stock
- pepper
- oil for drizzling
- fried shallots, spring onions and ginger strips to garnish

Condiments for serving with porridge:
- century eggs, quartered
- salted eggs, boiled, shelled and quartered
- rice vermicelli, deep-fried to a crisp
- prawn crackers

Marinate the pork with salt overnight. Just before cooking, rinse with water.

Marinate chicken meat with soya sauce overnight.

Cook the rice with the stock and the salted lean pork in a slow cooker. Start cooking at about 9pm over high heat. Just before going to bed, stir the porridge and scrape the bottom and change the setting to automatic or low. The next morning, give it another stir and scrape the bottom.

To make one serving, scoop a bowl of porridge into a small saucepan and bring to a simmer. Add a few pieces of marinated chicken and stir over medium heat until the chicken is cooked. Transfer into a bowl and drizzle with a little oil, garnish with fried shallots, spring onions and ginger strips. Season with soya sauce, salt and pepper. Serve with condiments on separate plates.

RICE DUMPLINGS
JUNG *(Makes about 16 dumplings)*

1	kg pork with some fat, cut into 2cm pieces
	salt
1	kg uncooked glutinous rice
300	g green split beans
	oil
2	tsp five-spice powder
1	tsp soya sauce
16	raw chestnuts, shelled and peeled
16	dried Chinese mushrooms, soaked; keep the water
½	tsp sugar
200	g lotus seeds, soaked and peeled, centres removed
200	g dried prawns, soaked and shelled
8	salted egg yolks, halved
35-40	bamboo leaves

Season the pork with salt and leave in the fridge overnight. Soak the glutinous rice and split beans separately.

The next day, rinse the pork with water. Heat a little oil in a wok and fry the pork with 1 teaspoon five-spice powder and a dash of soya sauce for a minute. The pork should be half-cooked.

Drain the rice. Add 1 level tablespoon salt and 1 tablespoon oil and mix thoroughly. Drain the split beans and add 1 teaspoon salt and 1 teaspoon oil and mix well.

Heat a little oil in a wok and stir-fry the chestnuts and mushroom with the soaking water, soya sauce, sugar and 1 teaspoon five-spice powder for a minute until the juices are almost dry.

Wrapping the dumplings: Blanch the bamboo leaves and dry them with a clean cloth. Use only the bigger, untorn leaves of equal width.

Place two leaves one on top of the other and spread the end slightly apart to form a narrow cross. Bend and twist the leaves in the middle to form a cone, with the tips and broad ends together.

Place a heaped tablespoon of rice into the cone, pressing the rice firmly into the corner. Make a hollow in the rice, pushing some rice up the sides of the cone. Place 1 heaped teaspoon of split beans in the hollow, making sure the beans are surrounded by the rice.

On top of the split beans, place 1 mushroom, 1 chestnut, half a yolk, 3-4 pieces of pork, 5-6 dried prawns, 5-6 lotus seeds. Top with 1 teaspoon of split beans. Scoop a tablespoon of rice on top and flatten the contents by pressing the ingredients tightly into the cone leaving a rim of leaves about ½cm along the edge of the cone.

Fold the long ends of the leaves down over the ingredients, fold them length-wise and twist them around the cone to form a tetrahedron, like a pyramid. Tie with a metre-long piece of raffia, leaving a long section for hanging.

Tie the raffia strips of 5 or 6 dumplings together to form a bunch.

Pack the dumplings into a large pot. Fill it with hot water to cover the dumplings. Cover the pot and boil over high heat for 2 hours, topping up with hot water every 30 minutes. Change the positions of the dumplings in the pot ever hour or so, moving those at the bottom to the top. Boil for another 2 hours, topping with water.

Lift the bundles of dumplings out of the water and hang them up to cool.

Tips

Green split beans are yellow as they have been skinned and halved.

For a more moist dumpling, include pieces of pork fat in the filling.

Variations

Alkaline Dumplings (Garn Shui Jung): These dumplings are bright yellow with translucent rice grains. They are either filled with red bean or have no filling, and both are often eaten dipped in sugar.

Make the dumplings as above but replace the pork filling with red bean paste which may be purchased ready-made. Before boiling the dumplings, add 3 tablespoons of alkaline water, also known as lye water, into the pot.

EGG NOODLES
MEEN

To make the noodles:

- 500 g bread flour
- 3 eggs, beaten
- 1 tsp alkaline water
- pinch of salt
- 5-6 tbs water
- starch for dusting

Put the flour into a large bowl and add the eggs, alkaline water and salt.

Combine the ingredients and knead the dough. Add the water one tablespoon at a time, kneading after each addition to distribute the moisture. Stop adding as soon as the dough leaves the bowl clean.

Transfer the dough onto a tabletop and knead it with the heel of the palm. It will still feel quite stiff and dry. The longer the dough is kneaded, the more springy the noodles.

Peel off a lump the size of a tennis ball. Flatten it into a thick disc and roll it through a pasta machine using the thickest setting. Dust both sides of the sheet with a little starch and repeat the rolling.

Roll repeatedly, using progressively thinner settings, twice per setting, making a long narrow sheet. Dust lightly with starch after each roll.

Finally, roll the dough sheet to make thin noodles. Catch the strands as they come out of the machine and roll them into a neat ball.

This portion makes about 10 balls of noodles.

To cook the noodles:

- 1 ball of uncooked noodles
- 2 tbs oyster sauce
- 1 tsp sesame oil
- ½ tsp soya sauce
- dash of pepper
- 2 tbs chicken stock

Bring a large pot of water to a rolling boil. Meanwhile, loosen a ball of noodles on a plate.

When the water is boiling, drop the noodles in and immediately stir and shake them about with a pair of chopsticks. After 10 seconds, scoop them up in a large wire ladle and hold them under cold running tap water for a few seconds. Return them to the boiling water for another few seconds.

Drain off most of the water and transfer to the plate with the seasoning. Immediately toss the noodles in the seasoning to mix well.

Serve with blanched green leafy vegetables and any meat you like.

Tips

Wrap each ball of noodles tightly with cling wrap and it can be kept frozen for a couple of months. Defrost overnight in the fridge in the wrapping before cooking.

P110/Rice & Noodles
RAT NOODLES
BAE TYE MUK

The alternative name in Cantonese is *low xu fun* or rat noodles because they look like the tails of rats.

- 1 cup water
- salt
- 500 g wheat starch, also known as dim sum flour

Pour the water into a large pot. Add a pinch of salt and bring the water to boil.

Pour the flour all at once into the pot and stir vigorously until the dough comes together in a lump. Remove from heat and cover a few seconds.

Transfer the hot dough onto a marble table. Rub oil onto the hands and knead the dough while it is still very hot, in the same way as kneading bread, pulling the dough and pushing it with the heel of the palm. Rub more oil onto the palms when the dough becomes sticky. The dough when done should be springy.

To make the noodles, pinch a small amount and roll it into a long round strand of about 0.3cm thick, pointed at both ends.

It can be fried with minced pork and bean sprouts, or used in noodle soup.

Savoury Snacks

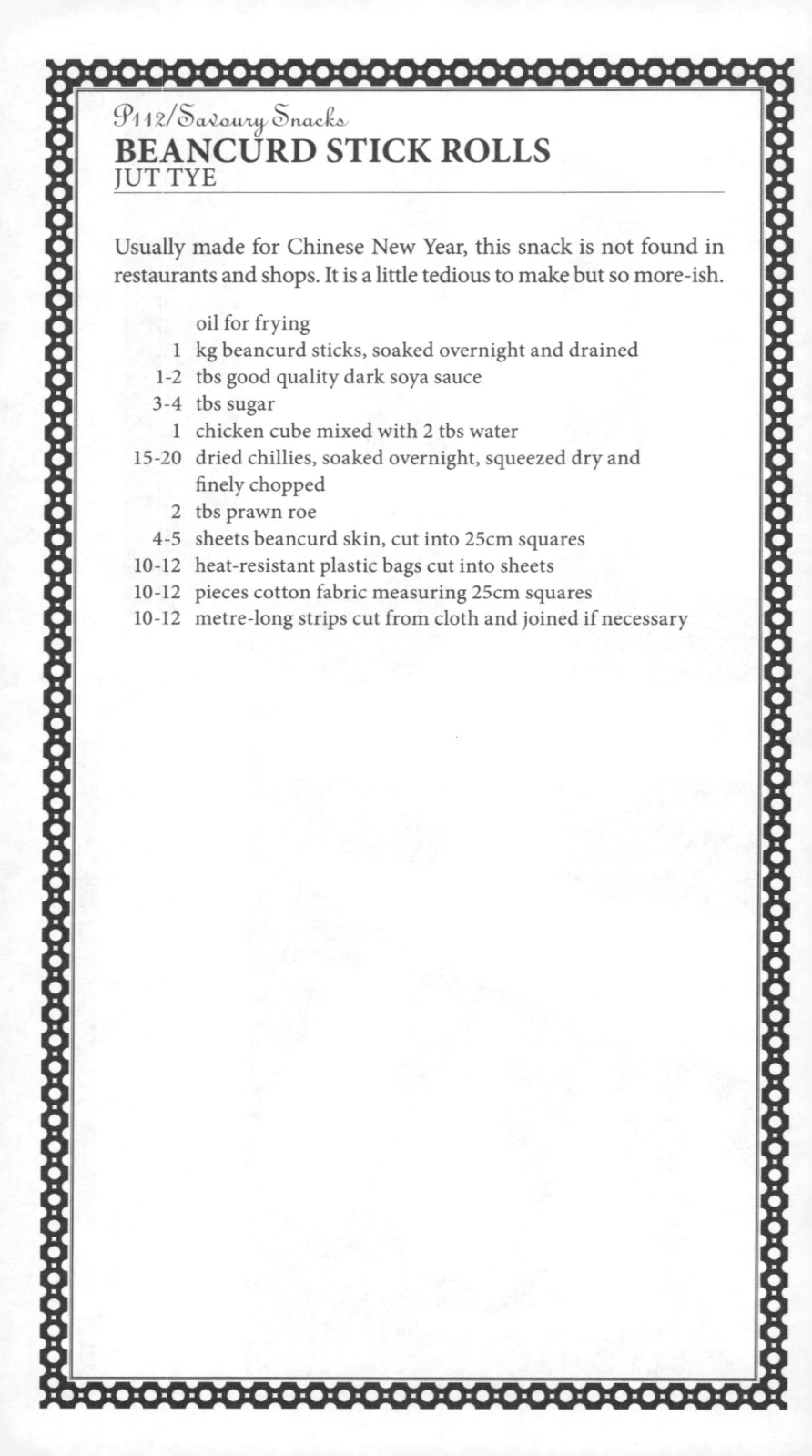

P112/Savoury Snacks
BEANCURD STICK ROLLS
JUT TYE

Usually made for Chinese New Year, this snack is not found in restaurants and shops. It is a little tedious to make but so more-ish.

	oil for frying
1	kg beancurd sticks, soaked overnight and drained
1-2	tbs good quality dark soya sauce
3-4	tbs sugar
1	chicken cube mixed with 2 tbs water
15-20	dried chillies, soaked overnight, squeezed dry and finely chopped
2	tbs prawn roe
4-5	sheets beancurd skin, cut into 25cm squares
10-12	heat-resistant plastic bags cut into sheets
10-12	pieces cotton fabric measuring 25cm squares
10-12	metre-long strips cut from cloth and joined if necessary

Fry the beancurd sticks, dark sauce, soya sauce, sugar and chicken cube water in a little oil. Stir-fry till almost dry. Taste the sauce and adjust with salt and sugar. The beancurd sticks should be dark brown.

Add the soaked chillies and prawn roe, and mix thoroughly. Transfer into a large pot and cool slightly.

Place a pile of sticks across one corner of a square of beancurd skin and wrap it tightly into a roll about 5cm thick and 15cm long. Wrap the roll in a plastic sheet.

Wrap tightly in a piece of cloth. Tie tightly with a strip of cloth along the entire length of the roll. Pull the strip as tightly as you can. Let the juices drip into a bowl for use in other dishes or discard it.

Steam the rolls for an hour. When cool, remove the cloth and plastic sheet. Cut diagonally into thin slices and serve.

Tips

Beancurd sheets are sold in large sheets. Wipe with a clean dry cloth before use.

Prawn roe looks like brown sand. It is sold in all dried seafood shops in Hong Kong, usually in 100g packets. Before using, stir-fry in a dry frying pan for about 5-10 minutes. Store in a tightly-sealed container in the fridge.

Use "Top" or "Superior" grade dark soya sauce.

P114/Savoury Snacks
YAM CAKE
WOO TAO GOU

- 600 g rice flour, Three Elephant brand
- 10 cups water
- oil for frying
- 100 g wax meat, diced, optional
- 1 Chinese sausage, diced
- 100 g dried prawns, soaked, shelled and finely chopped
- 1 yam, about 1kg, peeled and diced
- ½ tsp five-spice powder
- soya sauce
- salt and pepper
- pinch of sugar
- celery leaves to garnish

Mix the rice flour and water in a large bowl. Stir and mix by hand till smooth, squeezing the lumps to ensure thorough mixing.

Heat a little oil in a wok and stir-fry the wax meat, sausage, dried prawn and yam. Add five-spice powder and season with soya sauce, pepper, salt, and sugar to taste. Stir-fry for another minute or two.

Add the flour and water mixture and stir well until the mixture has thickened a little, but still with a pouring consistency.

Transfer into the pan that has been brushed with oil. Decorate with celery leaves and steam about 1 hour, until cooked.

Cut into 1cm thick slices and serve warm with chilli sauce. Or pan fry the slices till brown. Serve hot with chilli sauce.

Tips

The recipe is similar to that for radish cake except for the amount of water.
The pan may be round or square, but should be at least 6cm deep.
The chunks of yam, when cooked, should be soft like boiled potato.

Variation

A beaten egg may be added to the stir-fried slices.

P115/
RADISH CAKE
LOR BARK GOU

The cake should be soft but not starchy.

- 600 g rice flour, Three Elephant brand
- 9½ cups water, plus extra
- oil for frying
- 100 g wax meat, diced, optional
- 1 Chinese sausage, diced
- 100 g dried prawns, soaked, shelled and diced
- 1 kg radish, peeled and grated
- ½ tsp five-spice powder
- soya sauce
- salt and pepper
- pinch of sugar
- celery leaves to garnish

Mix the water with the rice flour in a large bowl. Stir and mix by hand till smooth, squeezing the lumps to ensure thorough mixing.

Heat a little oil in a wok and stir-fry the wax meat, sausage, prawn and radish and add the five-spice powder. Season with soya sauce, pepper, salt, and sugar to taste. Stir-fry for another minute or two.

Add the flour and water mixture and stir-fry, stirring well until the mixture has thickened a little, but still with a pouring consistency.

Transfer into the pan that has been brushed with oil. Top with celery leaves and steam about 1 hour, until cooked.

Cut into 1cm thick slices and serve warm with chilli sauce. Or pan fry the slices till brown. Serve hot with chilli sauce.

Tips

The recipe is similar to that for yam cake except for the amount of water.
The pan may be round or square, but should be at least 6cm deep.

Variation

A beaten egg may be added to the stir-fried slices if you like.

P116/Savoury Snacks
CHINESE POTATO CRISPS
CHAR PAU

This vegetable, which looks like a yellow water chestnut, is also called Chinese arrowroot, but in the wet market, it is called *chi goo* in Cantonese. To complicate things, when sliced and deep-fried, it is called *char pau*.

A Chinese New Year goodie, *char pau* actually is a mixture of *chi goo* crisps, crisps of yam and sweet potato and roasted peanuts. But we don't bother with the rest.

- 2 kg Chinese arrowroot, washed and peeled, with the stalks intact
  oil for deep-frying
  salt

Holding the stalk, slice the bulb thinly, about 1-2mm thick, with a mandoline.

Heat enough oil in a wok for deep-frying over medium heat. Drop the slices into the oil one at a time – not a handful at a time as they will stick together and become soggy. Fry no more than 6-8 slices at a time or they will be difficult to control and burn easily. Remove when golden and drain. Dust with salt if desired and keep in a tightly-sealed tin. Adjust the heat if the slices brown too quickly.

Variation

To make the original version of char pau, besides Chinese arrowroot, cut a sweet potato and a yam into 2mm slices and cut the slices into diamond shapes. Deep-fry till golden brown. Sweet potato and yam slices can be fried in small handfuls as they separate easily when stirred in the hot oil. Deep-fry 200g large skinless peanuts for 2-3 minutes till golden. Mix all the crisps and peanuts and serve.

An aunt used to slice the chi goo by hand into 3-4mm thick slices and sun-dry them before deep-frying. The result is a crisp with more bite, which some people prefer to the light crisp of thin slices. Also, some of the dried slices would puff up in a ball when fried, which is quite nice.

Shopping list

Guest list

Desserts

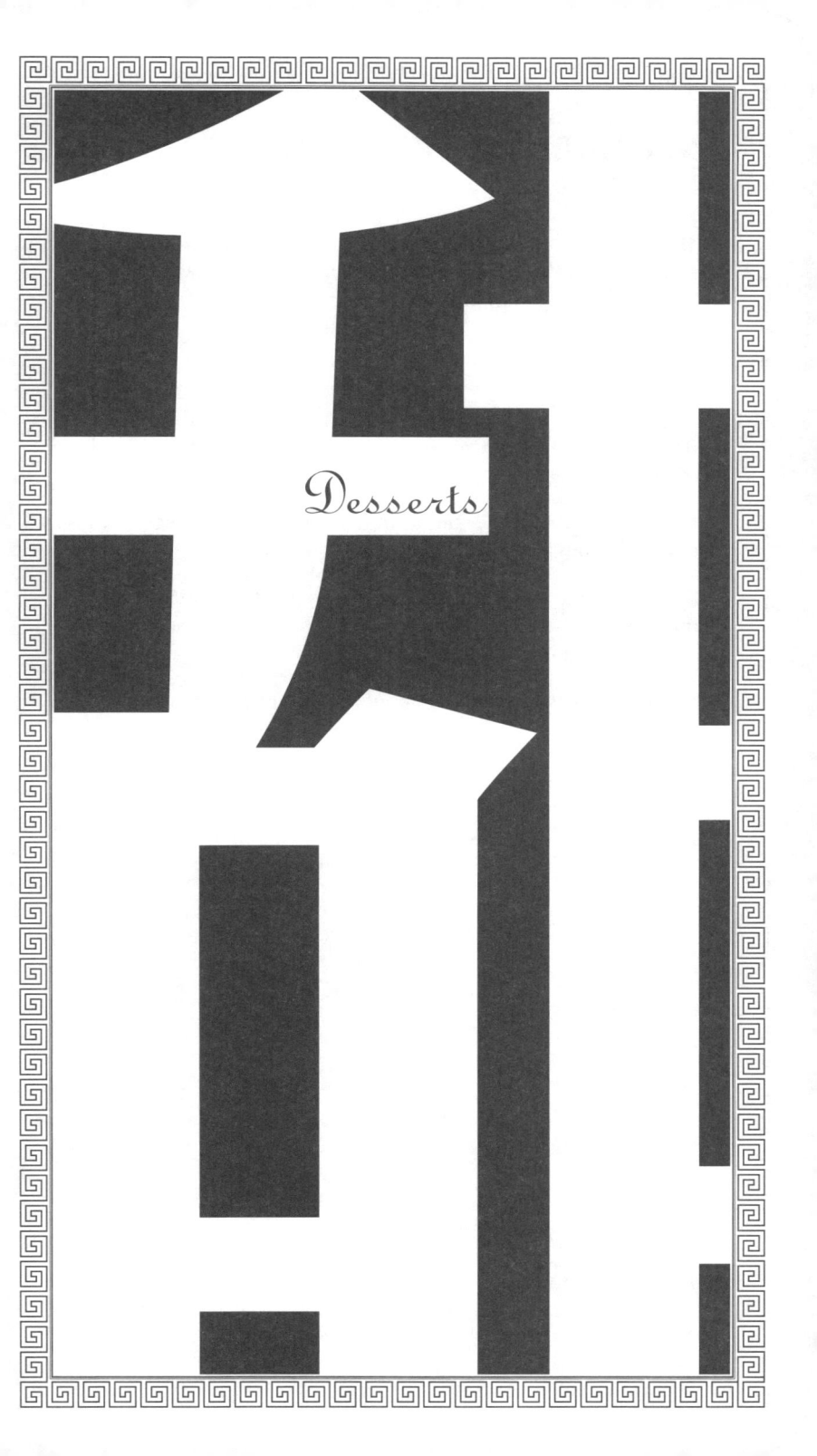

STEAMED EGG CUSTARD
JENG DARN

This is a lovely and light dessert. Mother would make it for tea, which used to be an elaborate affair, usually as a break during Sunday mahjong sessions.

- 2 eggs
- water
- 2 tbs sugar

Break the eggs into a measuring cup. Note the volume and transfer to a big bowl.

Measure out double the volume in water and add to the egg. Beat to mix thoroughly.

Add the sugar and stir until completely melted. Pour the egg mix through a sieve and into small bowls. Be sure to scoop out any bubbles along the edges.

Steam over very low heat for about 8-10 minutes. Serve hot.

Tips

It is important not to over-cook the custard or it will lose the smooth texture crucial in egg custard. Check after 8 minutes. The centre of the surface should still be slightly wobbly. Turn off the heat and leave the bowls in the steamer under cover to finish the cooking. Check again after a minute or so.

The number of servings depends on the size of the bowls. It is best to use small bowls as it is difficult to get the egg to cook evenly if the bowl is too deep.

ℛ121/
RED BEANS SOUP
HOONG DAU SUI

The Cantonese is well known for their numerous sweet soups (*tong sui*). This is just one of them. In many dim sum restaurants, this is often made with insufficient beans, or too starchy, or too sweet. At home, you can control all three. We like ours with lots of beans.

- 600 g red beans, washed and soaked overnight
- 2-3 pieces dried tangerine skin, washed, optional
- 5-6 tbs sugar
- water
- coconut milk, optional

Transfer the beans and tangerine skin into a large pot and add 2-3 tablespoons sugar and enough water to cover the beans by about 6cm. Bring to boil and simmer over medium heat until the beans are soft and cracked open, about an hour or more. Add water if the liquid reduces too much.

Add more sugar to desired sweetness. Just before serving, drizzle with coconut milk.

Variations

The husk of the beans is removed to make a more refined version known as hung dao sar meaning "red bean sand". After the beans are soft, transfer the beans to a sieve placed over the pot of sweet soup. Mash the beans with a spoon. Pour some sweet soup through the sieve and "wash" the mashed beans through the sieve into the pot, leaving the husk in the sieve.

To thicken the soup slightly, mix 2 tablespoons of glutinous rice flour with 2 tablespoons of water and stir into the simmering soup a little at a time, stirring constantly. Stop when the soup thickens to the desired consistency. Before serving, drizzle with coconut milk.

The red beans may be replaced by green beans.

BLACK SESAME SOUP
JEE MAH WOO

- 250 g black sesame seeds
- 1 tsp white sesame seeds
- 5 tbs sugar
- 1 tbs glutinous rice flour

Combine the black and white sesame seeds and wash in a sieve, letting water run through slowly, stirring the seeds with your hands. Drain.

Stir-fry over medium-low heat until the white seeds turn yellowish brown. Be careful not to burn the seeds.

Transfer to a pot with enough water just to cover the seeds. Process the seeds and water in a blender until fine.

Push the blended seeds through a metal sieve and discard the shells. Then push the sieved seeds through a piece of muslin cloth and discard the debris. What's left is a smooth fine watery paste.

Transfer to a pot and add the glutinous rice flour. Mix well by breaking up the lumps. Add sugar to taste. Simmer while stirring continuously.

P123/
LOTUS SEEDS SOUP
LEEN JEE TONG SUI

- 200 g lotus seeds, soaked and peeled, centres removed
- 4 tbs sugar
- 4 cups water
- 6-8 quail's eggs, hard-boiled and shelled, optional

Place the lotus seeds into a pot with 3 tablespoons sugar and the water. Simmer for an hour or longer until the seeds are soft and sweet. Adjust the sweetness of the soup to taste.

Add the quail's eggs to the lotus seeds soup.

Tips

The best lotus seeds come with the skin and the green shoots in tact. But skinless seeds are now available, although there're always bits of green shoots left inside which must be removed as they are bitter.

Often, the lotus seeds served in restaurants and hawker stalls are crunchy and tasteless. It is important that the lotus seeds are soft and sweet which means simmering with sugar for quite a long time.

Variations

Instead of quail's eggs, you may use 2 chicken eggs. Beat the eggs with a couple of tablespoons of the sweet soup. Bring the soup to boil and add the egg mixture while stirring so the egg is cooked in strands.

Gingko nuts may be added to the soup.

DOUBLE-BOILED SNOW FUNGUS
DUN SHUIT YEE

- 50 g snow fungus, soaked and cleaned
- 2 lumps rock sugar, about 3cm each
- 2 cups water
- 6-8 quail's eggs, hard-boiled and shelled, optional

Break the clumps of snow fungus into pieces and simmer in water for a minute. Discard the water.

Transfer to a double-boiler. Add the rock sugar and water. Cook for 1-2 hours until the fungus is soft, but still has a crunch.

Add the quail's eggs. Serve hot.

Tips

Be sure to buy the yellowish, dry snow fungus, sold in clumps like flowers.

If you do not have a double-boiler, you can simmer the mixture over very low heat or use a slow cooker.

ℛ125/
JADE DESSERT
BEK YOKE KENG JIONG

This is not found in any restaurant and Mother does not remember where she learned it.

- 1 can green peas, about 400g
- 3 cups water
- 20 strands agar agar, soaked
- 3 tbs sugar
- ¼ cup freshly-squeezed coconut milk

Pour peas into a metal sieve and mash them with a spoon. Push the mashed peas through the sieve and discard the shells.

Transfer the mashed peas to a pot with 3 cups water and bring to boil. Drain the agar agar strips and add to the pot. Simmer until most of the agar agar has dissolved and the liquid has thickened a little. Add more water if it becomes too thick. Strain the liquid through a sieve again to remove any undissolved agar agar bits. Add 3 tablespoons sugar or more to the desired sweetness.

Just before serving, bring the liquid to a simmer and drizzle the coconut milk to make a swirl on the surface.

Tips

Be sure to buy peas that are bright green in colour, such as the Ayam brand peas.

It is easier to mash the peas if you remove the shells by squeezing each pea gently between two fingers to make the inside pops out.

The pea soup will set when it cools but still soft enough to stir and mix it into a liquid again when warming up to serve. If the pea liquid is too thick, or too much agar agar is used, it will set into a firm jelly.

P126/Desserts
SWEET POTATO SOUP
FARN SHUE TONG SUI

- 500 g sweet potatoes, orange or purple variety, peeled
- 4 tbs sugar
- 3-4 cups water
- 2 cm piece of ginger, peeled and sliced, optional

Cut the sweet potatoes into 2cm cubes. Place into a pot with the sugar, water and the ginger slices, if using.

Bring to boil and simmer till soft, about 20 minutes. Do not over boil or the cubes will break up.

℘127/
GINGKO NUTS WITH SOYA BEAN STICKS
FOO JOKE BARK GOR

- 100 g beancurd sticks, soaked
- 200 g gingko nuts, shelled and peeled
- 2 tbs pearl barley, washed and soaked
- 4 tbs sugar
- tiny pinch of baking soda or a few drops of alkaline water

Cut the soaked beancurd sticks into 6cm sections.

Transfer into a big pot with the gingko nuts, barley, and 2 tablespoons sugar. Add water to cover by about 6cm. Simmer uncovered over medium heat for about an hour until the gingko nuts are soft and sweet. Half way through, add the baking soda or alkaline water. Add more water if necessary. Simmer till the beancurd sticks are soft.

Adjust sweetness to taste.

GLUTINOUS RICE BALLS
TONG YUEN

A must for Chinese New Year, the balls are said to resemble eggs, which signify fertility.

- 6 tbs sugar
- 4 cups water
- 2-3 slices of ginger, optional
- 600 g glutinous rice flour, Three Elephant brand
- gula melaka, cut into ½cm pieces

Make a sweet soup by simmering 4 tablespoons sugar in 3 cups of water, and the ginger slices if using, for 10 minutes. Set aside.

Place the flour into a large bowl and add half the water slowly while stirring. Keep adding a little at a time until the flour comes together in a ball. Knead the dough till smooth.

Scoop a teaspoon of the dough and roll into a 2cm ball, dusting hands with glutinous flour. Flatten it and push a small piece of gula melaka inside and enclose it in the dough. Roll the ball in glutinous rice flour.

Bring a large pot of water to boil and add 2 tablespoons sugar. Lower the balls into the simmering water a few at a time. When they float, they are done. Remove from water and transfer into the pot of sweet soup.

To serve, scoop 5 rice balls into a small bowl and fill with sweet soup.

Variation

Traditionally, the balls are filled with lumps of orange-coloured sugar, sold in slabs. But gula melaka is more fragrant.

𝒫129/
SOYA MILK
DAU SUI

This is easily available in hawker stalls, but homemade soya milk is unbeatable.

- 500 g soya beans, washed and soaked overnight
- 8 cups water
- 3 tbs sugar

Drain the beans and blend finely with half the water.

Transfer the blended mixture into a large muslin bag. Tie it up tightly and wring out the milk into a pot. Place the bag into a pot and pour the remaining water into the bag. Twist the bag closed, knead the bean pulp and squeeze the liquid into the pot.

Bring the pot of soya milk to boil and turn off as soon as it starts to simmer or it will boil over. Add sugar to taste.

Tip

Add more water if you prefer the milk to be more dilute.

WATER CHESTNUT CAKE
MAR TYE GOU

- 4 cups water
- 150 g water chestnut flour
- 1 cup sugar
- 300 g raw water chestnuts, peeled and diced

Pour 2 cups of water into a bowl with the water chestnut flour. Stir till smooth.

Boil the other 2 cups of water with sugar until dissolved and reduce the heat. Add the flour mixture to the syrup. Stir vigorously into a thick starch. Add the diced water chestnut and stir to mix well.

Transfer into a shallow pan and steam 30 minutes or longer. The batter will still be soft but will set when cool. Keep in the fridge. Cut into ½cm thick slices, fry in a little oil and serve hot.

P131/
NEW YEAR CAKE
LEEN GOU

Mother has modified this traditional cake with local flavours.

- 400 g gula melaka
- 2 cups water
- 600 g glutinous rice flour, Three Elephant brand
- 200 g castor sugar, plus extra 1 tbs
- milk from 1 coconut
- 3 tins, about 10cm in diameter and 5cm deep, lined with plastic sheets cut from plastic bags

Dissolve the gula melaka and sugar in 2 cups of simmering water in a pot over medium heat. When all the sugar has dissolved, pour the liquid through a sieve to remove the impurities.

Mix the coconut milk with the gula melaka liquid to make about 3 cups of liquid.

Place flour into a large pot. Add a tablespoon of sugar and mix well. Add the coconut milk ½ cup at a time and stir after each addition till smooth. The final mixture should be quite thick but can still be poured.

Pour the batter into the prepared tins about 80 percent full. Steam over medium low heat for 4 hours.

Cool completely before removing from the tins. Trim the edge of the cake and the plastic sheet, wrap tightly and keep in the fridge.

To serve, cut into ½cm thick slices and fry in a little oil till brown. Add a beaten egg and fry till the egg is cooked.

Alternatively, cut into ½cm thick slices, steam to warm through, coat with grated coconut and serve.

Tip

Mother used to line the tins with banana leaves but the batter would leak. Plastic sheets work much better.

HASMA SWEET SOUP
SHUIT GARP TONG SUI

This is the reproductive organ of frogs and is supposed to nourish the respiratory system and lungs. Definitely an acquired taste.

- 200 g hasma, soaked and cleaned
- 2-3 lumps rock sugar, about 3cm each
- 1 egg, lightly beaten or 3-4 quail's eggs, hard-boiled and shelled

Simmer the hasma in water for 1-2 minutes. Drain and discard water.

Simmer the rock sugar in 2-3 cups water until the sugar is dissolved. Add the hasma.

Lightly beat the egg with 2 tablespoons water, and stir into the simmering sweet soup. Alternatively, add several hard-boiled quail's eggs.

Shopping list

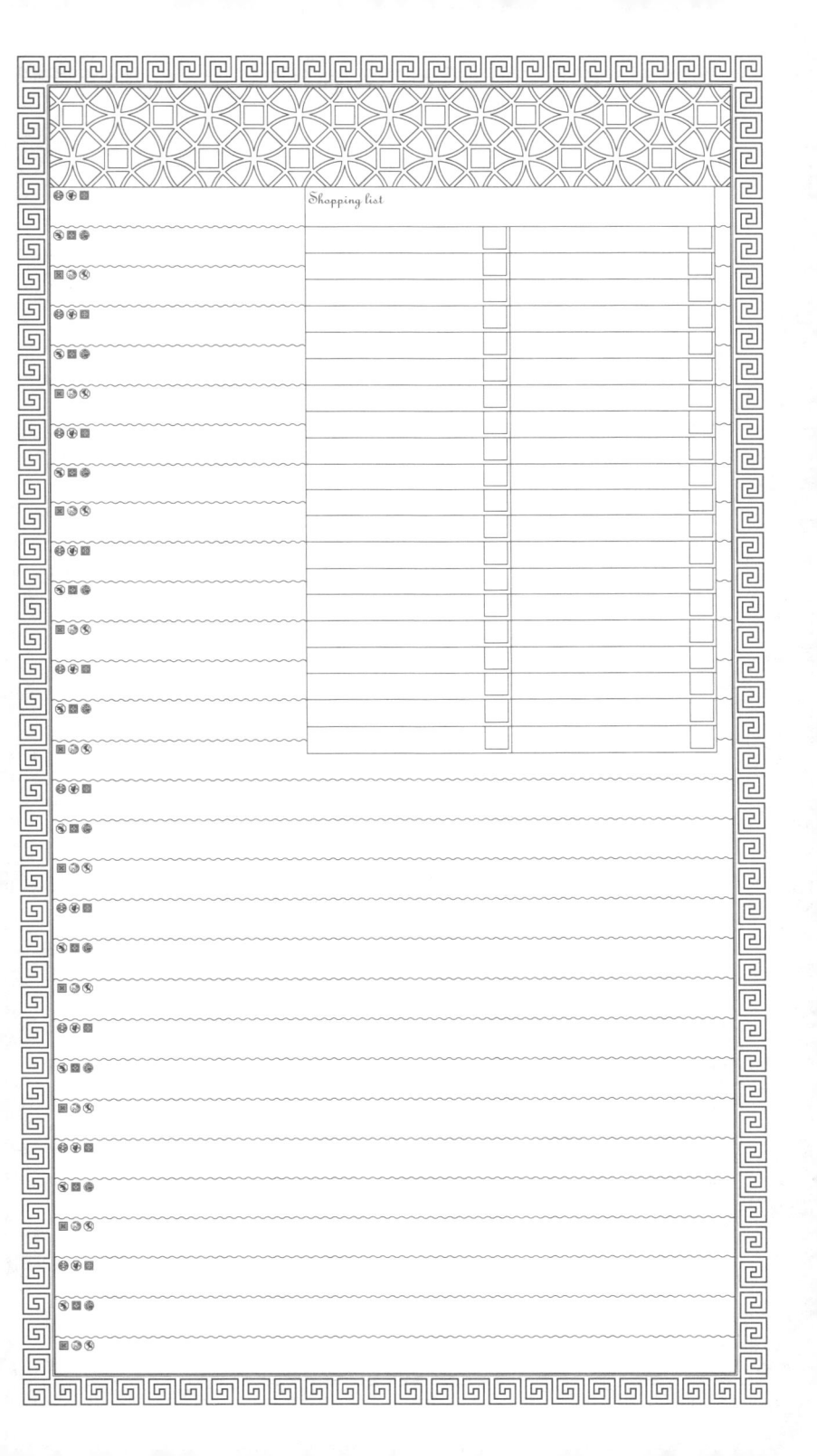

Guest list

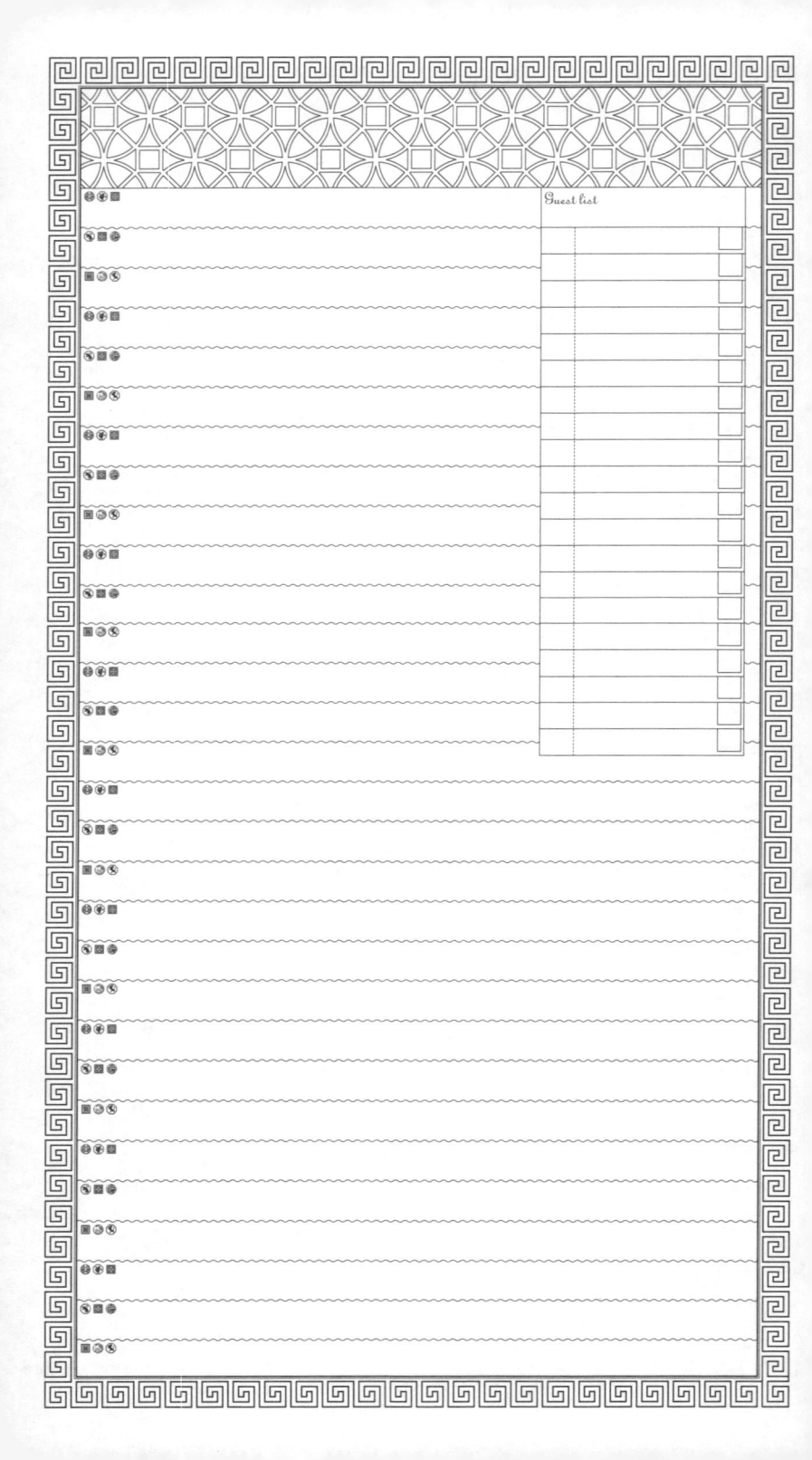

Actual size

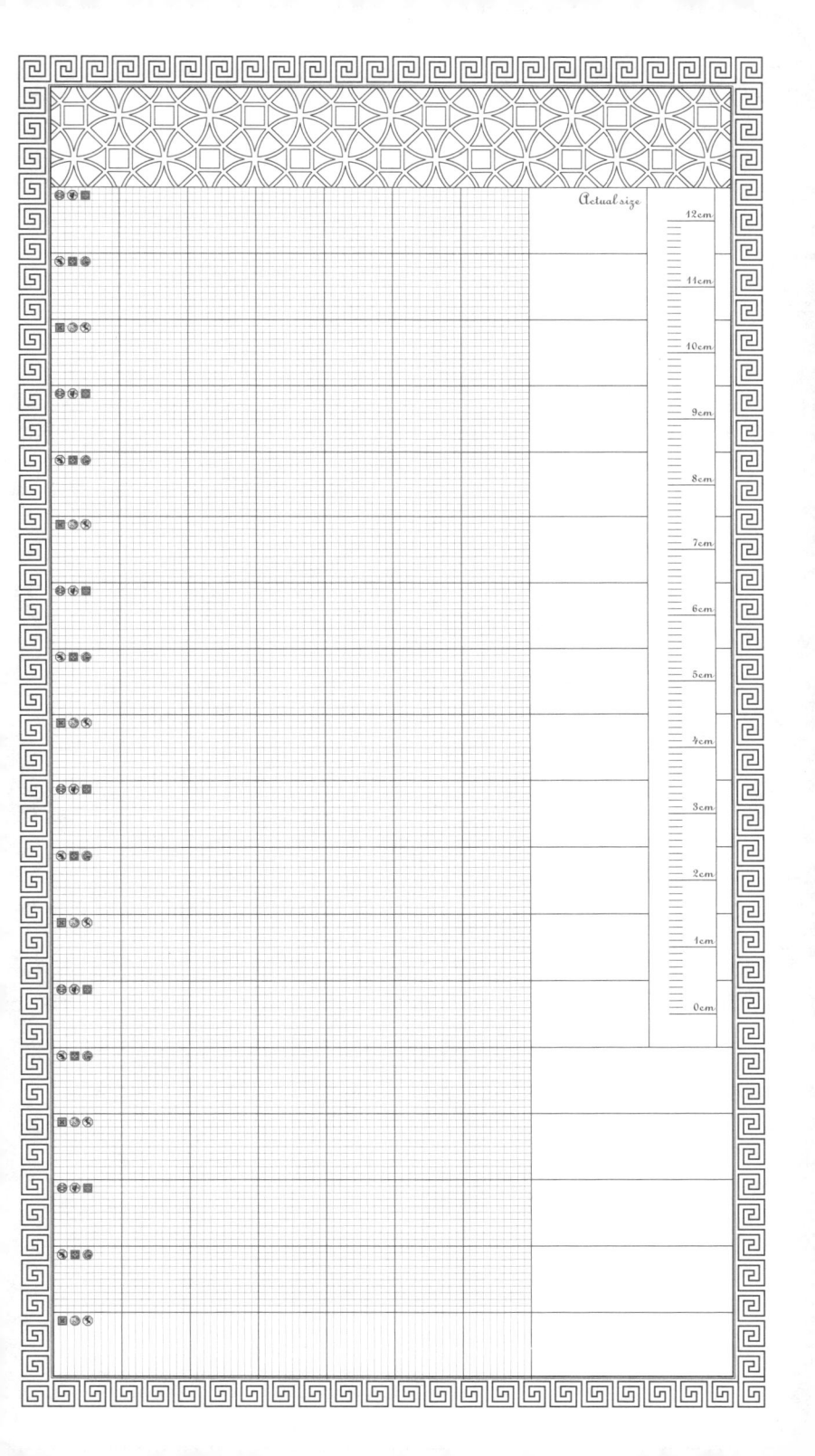

12cm
11cm
10cm
9cm
8cm
7cm
6cm
5cm
4cm
3cm
2cm
1cm
0cm

Glossary

Ingredient	Cantonese Name	Ingredient	Cantonese Name
abalone	*bau yu*	duck	*ngarp*
alkaline water	*garn shui*	duck gizzards	*lup ngarp sun*
astragalus	*buk kay*	egg	*darn*
bamboo fungus	*joke sun*	ferox nuts	*see sut*
barbeque pork	*char siew*	fish	*yu*
batang fish	*gau yu*	fish maw	*yu tou*
beancurd	*dau foo*	fish slices	*yu peen*
beancurd skin	*foo pae*	five-spice powder	*ng heong fun*
beancurd sticks	*foo joke*	flower mushroom	*far goo*
bell peppers	*dung loong jiu*	garoupa	*sek barn*
bird's nest	*yeen wor*	ginger	*geong*
bitter gourd	*foo gua*	gingko nuts	*bark gor*
black vinegar	*hark choe*	ginseng	*yong sum*
boxthorn	*gau gae*	ginseng beard	*yong sum soe*
broccoli	*gye larn far*	glutinous rice, uncooked	*lor mye*
carrots	*hoong lor bark*	glutinous rice, cooked	*lor mye farn*
chicken	*gye*	green beans	*loke dau*
chicken feet	*gye geok*	hair seaweed or hair fungus	*fatt choy*
Chinese broccoli	*gye larn*	hairy marrow	*jeet gua*
Chinese cabbage	*wong ngar bark*	ham	*for toi*
Chinese chives	*gau choy*	hasma	*shuit garp*
Chinese cooking wine	*far diu*	lettuce	*sarng choy*
Chinese kam wah ham	*for toei*	lily bulbs	*bark hup*
Chinese mushrooms	*doong goo*	lotus root	*leen ngau*
Chinese potato	*chi goo*	lotus seeds	*leen jee*
Chinese sausage	*larp cheong*	mustard greens	*choy sum*
Chinese spinach	*bor choy*	old cucumber	*lou wong gua*
clams	*heen*	old ginger	*lou geong*
cloud-ear fungus	*wun yee*	oyster sauce	*hou yau*
congee	*joke*	pearl barley	*yee mye*
cordyceps	*doong choong choe*	pig's brain	*ju nou*
crabs	*hie*	pig's caul	*ju mong yaw*
cuttlefish	*diu peen*	pig's liver	*ju yuen*
dioscorea	*wye sarn*	pig's stomach	*ju tou*
dried beancurd	*teem joke*	pig's trotters	*ju geok*
dried prawns	*har mye*	pomfret	*chong yu*
dried scallops	*gong yu chi*	pork	*ju yoke*
dried lily bulbs	*bark hup*	pork ribs	*pye guat*
dried longan	*longan yoke*	potato	*shu jye*
dried squid	*jiong yu*		

Ingredient	Cantonese Name
prawn paste	*har jeong*
prawn roe	*har jee*
radish	*lor bark*
red beans	*hoong dau*
red dates	*hoong jou*
rice, uncooked	*jeem mye*
rice, cooked	*farn*
rice dumplings	*jung*
rice flour	*jeem mye fun*
rice vermicelli	*mye fun*
salted fish	*harm yu*
salted pickled mustard greens	*harm choy*
sea cucumber	*hoi sum*
sesame oil	*mah yau*
sesame seeds, black	*hark jee mah*
sesame seeds, white	*bark jee mah*
silver pomfret	*dau dye*
snakehead fish	*sarng yu*
snow fungus	*shuit yee*
snow peas	*shuit dau*
soya milk	*dau sui*
spring onions	*choong*
sweet almond	*nam hung*
sweet potato	*farn shue*
Szechuan pepper	*far jeu*
threadfin or ikan kurau	*mah yau*
top shells	*hiong lor*
vermicelli	*fun see*
water chestnut	*mar tye*
watercress	*sye yong choy*
wax meat	*larp yoke*
wheat starch	*dung meen*
winter melon	*doong gua*
wolfberries	*gae jee*
wood-ear fungus	*mook yee*
yam	*woo tau*

As a guide

½ tsp = 2.5ml   ½ cup = 100ml
1 tsp = 5ml   1 cup = 200ml
½ tbs = 7.5ml   1 cup sugar = 150g
1 tbs = 15ml

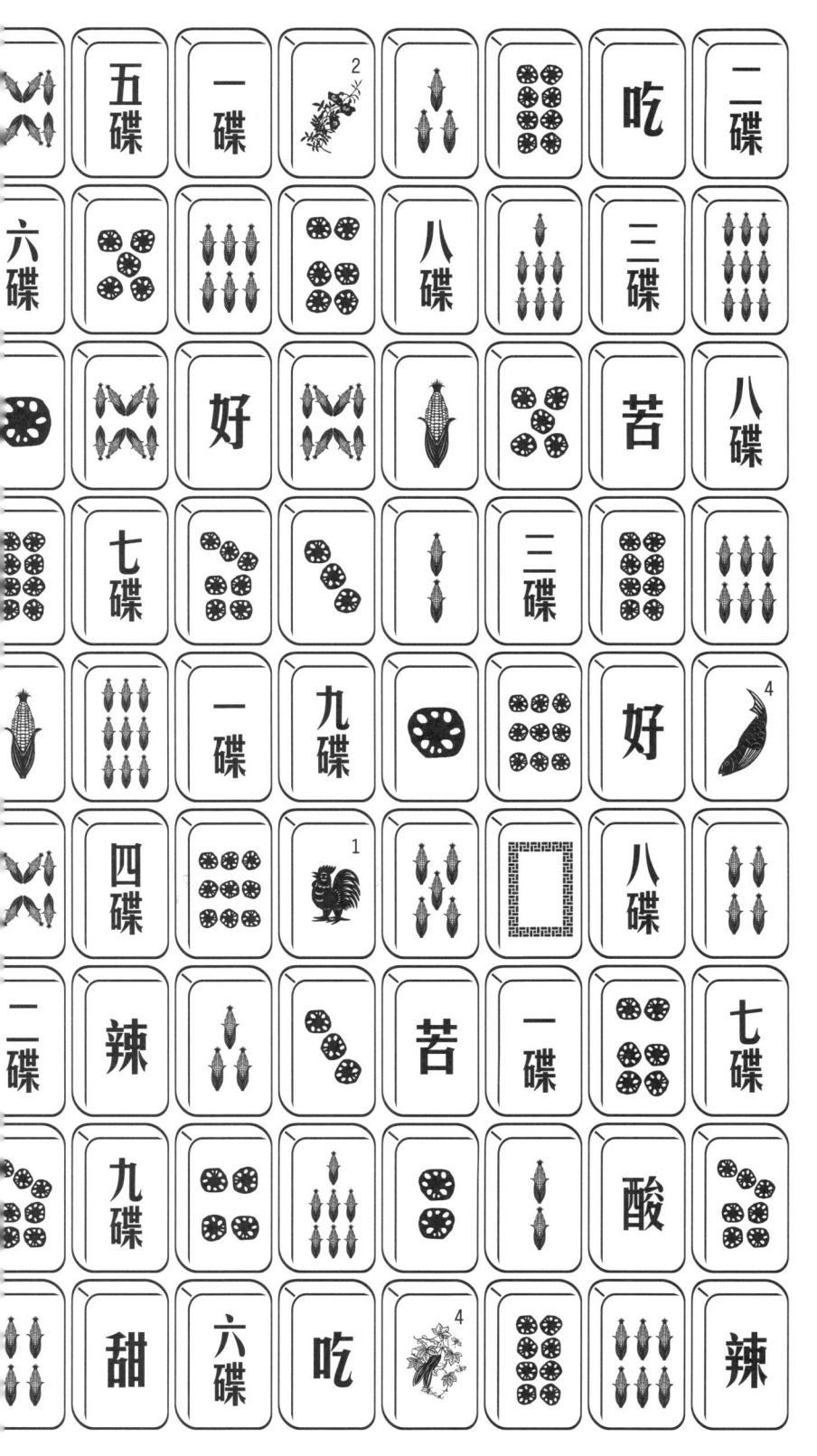

	五碟	一碟				吃	二碟
六碟				八碟		三碟	
		好				苦	八碟
	七碟				三碟		
		一碟	九碟			好	
	四碟					八碟	
二碟	辣			苦	一碟		七碟
	九碟					酸	
	甜	六碟	吃				辣

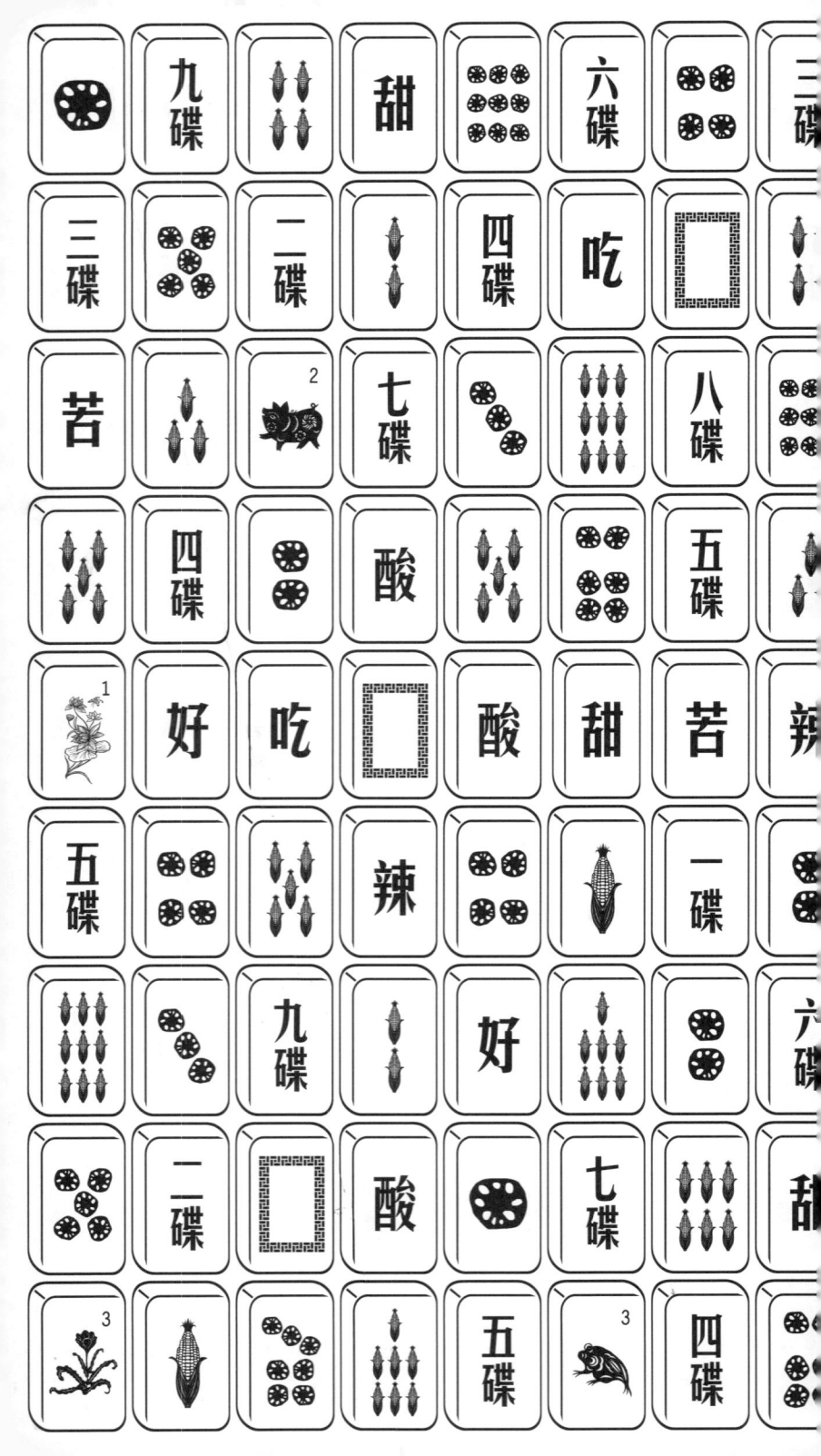

🪷	九碟	🌽🌽	甜	⚫⚫⚫⚫⚫⚫⚫	六碟	⚫⚫⚫⚫	三碟
三碟	⚫⚫⚫⚫⚫	一碟	🌽	四碟	吃	口	🌽
苦	🌽🌽	🐷2	七碟	⚫⚫⚫	🌽🌽🌽🌽	八碟	⚫⚫⚫⚫⚫⚫
🌽🌽🌽	四碟	⚫	酸	🌽🌽🌽	⚫⚫⚫⚫	五碟	🌽
🌸1	好	吃	口	酸	甜	苦	辣
五碟	⚫⚫⚫⚫	🌽🌽🌽	辣	⚫⚫⚫⚫⚫	🌽	一碟	⚫⚫⚫
🌽🌽🌽🌽🌽🌽	⚫⚫⚫	九碟	🌽	好	🌽🌽🌽🌽	⚫	六碟
⚫⚫⚫⚫	二碟	口	酸	⚫⚫	七碟	🌽🌽🌽	甜
🌸3	🌽	⚫⚫⚫⚫⚫	🌽🌽🌽	五碟	🐸3	四碟	⚫⚫⚫